INTO OURSELVES
An Exploration into the Human Experience

By

James Sinclair

ISBN 13: 978-1511462976
ISBN: 1511462973

Acknowledgments

For cover images, credit goes to:

© http://kuschelirmel-stock.deviantart.com/ For the Background Pyramid Image

© Jimmyi23 | Dreamstime.com - Human Evolution Photo

© Skalapendra | Dreamstime.com - Gender Brain Photo

Table of Contents

Ares
Aphrodite

Heroes, Legends, and Myths
Ulysses
Hercules
Samson
David
Robin Hood
King Arthur
Aladdin and his Lamp
Sinbad the Sailor
Superman
Batman
Spiderman
Doctor Who
Dragons
Fairies
Santa Claus
Count Dracula
Werewolves
Zombies
Ghosts

Where We Live

Explorers, Navigators, and Colonisers

Builders and Constructors
Buildings
Roads and Railways
Bridges
Tunnels
Canals
Ship Building

The Ascent of Man

Out of Africa

Before the dawning of the 19th century, most of the early history of humans on this planet came from accounts given in the Bible in the book of Genesis. There was a general belief that man had been created by the hand of God as part of His divine creation of the Universe. Of course, there were different creation stories in Africa, India, and China, and amongst many native peoples—like the American Indian. As far as dating the past was concerned, taking into account the generations listed in the Old Testament, it was thought that the creation of the Earth took place in 4004 B.C. (worked out by James Usher in the 17th century), and this date can be seen in the margins of printed copies of the old Authorised version of the Bible. Since then, finds by archaeologists and anthropologists have dated the history of early man back to about 2.5 million years, when our ape-like ancestors roamed the prairies of Africa.

These early hominids wandered around in small groups, hunting whatever prey they could kill with their primitive weapons, or scavenging for food and gathering what edible plants were available to eat. They must have been very vulnerable to attack by the ferocious carnivores of their day that preyed upon them.

In time to come, early humans developed larger brains, and by about 1.5 million years ago, were fashioning efficient tools. It is thought they also mastered the art of making fire to provide warmth and light, and also to prepare cooked food.

These early humans had the intelligence to plan hunting expeditions and bring their kills back to fixed camps, where they lived in groups.

Evolutionary changes continued to take place: children took longer to reach adulthood, and women had to devote more of their time to child rearing. Within each small group, social interactions were necessary and a means of communication much needed, such as development of early language. However, full speech capability is thought to have evolved some 0.5 million years ago in the later stages of human evolution, but no one knows exactly when this happened.

The early ancestors of man first started to migrate from his African home perhaps 2 million years ago, and spread through Europe, Asia and eventually across the globe.

Into Egypt

As the last Ice Age came to an end, some 12,000 years ago, man's development progressed under more favourable conditions. At that time, parts of the Sahara desert were green and fertile, and early cave paintings depicted men hunting animal species like elephants, buffalos, and antelopes. No one really knows for sure when these early people moved to this region, but stone circles, barrow graves, and ancient settlement sites have been discovered by archaeologists, which indicate that early humans indeed inhabited this area at one time. These ancient Stone Age people learned how to domesticate and herd animals, and made the change from hunter-gatherers to farmers, growing crops of early varieties of wheat and barley.

It is not quite clear when religious thought first began, but with burial rituals it is clear that thoughts about a spiritual world were developing, and later, when the growing of crops was at the mercy of the elements—rain or drought—man turned to gods and deities who seemed to be in control of these events, and ritual offerings, to appease these gods and deities, started in earnest.

Farming took off in settlements on the banks of the river Nile in Egypt in the centuries before 5,000 years B.C. Over the course of the next two millennia, fortified villages and towns took shape, and the communities built up until they numbered up to several thousand. Eventually, two main kingdoms emerged, one in Upper Egypt and the other in Lower Egypt, but these finally merged into one kingdom. The city of Memphis at the head of the Nile delta was to become the principal home of the Pharaohs for almost 1,500 years, until it was replaced by Thebes, on the Nile's upper course.

Under the leadership of a Pharaoh, a form of government was established, and the Pharaoh himself was given a semi-divine status, becoming a god after his death. To facilitate governing the people and collecting taxes, a written language was developed with pictorial scripts, known as hieroglyphs, being carved on monuments. A more simplified script known as hieratic was preferred for daily use, like drawing up tax accounts. Scribes had to be especially trained in the art of writing, and this was done by engraving the characters on clay tablets, then later with a pen made from a sharpened reed, and ink made from ground earth-pigments to allow the writing of characters on scrolls of papyrus.

The period of pyramid building commenced with the building of the Stepped Pyramid around about 2500 B.C., followed by the building of other pyramids. The greatest of these being the Great Pyramid at Giza, the largest of a group of three pyramids in a line, with the one at the end slightly out of alignment with the other two. There are theories that this was deliberately done to represent the three stars in the belt of the constellation of Orion, where the end star is slightly out of alignment. It is hard to understand why the Egyptians considered it necessary to build such colossal structures merely as a tomb for the Pharaoh, as it must have required a labour force of thousands to carve, lift, and manoeuver these massive blocks of stone, and raise them to the top of a very high structure—the tallest in the world at the time. It is still astonishing to archaeologists today as to the logistics of this enormous undertaking, as besides the labour force required, very skilled and precise mathematics were used to build these massive structures so perfectly. These pyramids were designed to house the mummified remains of the Pharaohs and all their treasures, to accompany them into the after world.

The ancient Egyptians worshipped many gods and deities, some of which took the form of half-animal, half-human depictions, like the jackal god and the crocodile god. By the fifth dynasty, they had begun to worship the Sun God, Ra. Their religion was well organised with temples, priests, altars where offerings of food, water, and flowers were left to provide refreshment for the gods, and the performing of religious rituals. There is no evidence that human or animal sacrifices were made to the gods, although it is thought that, in earlier times, the administrators and servants of the Pharaoh were killed and buried with him in order to serve him in the after world. It was the belief of the ancient Egyptians that the afterlife was a continuation of the worldly life, so therefore the dead, especially in the case of someone important like a Pharaoh, would need all their worldly goods and possessions to continue to live in comfort in the afterlife. In addition, they needed a body to return to, from time to time, and therefore their bodies were mummified and preserved in their tombs.

It may come as a surprise, but very little was known about the ancient Egyptians until Napoleon invaded Egypt at the end of the 18th century. Even the Great Sphinx near the Pyramids of Giza was half buried in the sand, with only its head showing, until excavations were made by a team of archaeologists who accompanied Napoleon and his soldiers. In addition, the hieroglyphic inscriptions on the various monuments were indecipherable, and it was only with the discovery of the Rosetta Stone that these hieroglyphs could be interpreted. This stone was inscribed with Egyptian hieroglyphic writing and a translation in Greek, and in 1822 a Frenchman, Jean-Francois Champollion, used his knowledge of Greek to compare the texts and was able to work out what the ancient Egyptian writings said. From that day, we were able to read the hieroglyphs on ancient Egyptian monuments, and our knowledge of ancient Egypt increased a hundredfold. Before that, we had little knowledge of the history of that ancient civilization.

The Church, however, was concerned about the discovery of the Rosetta Stone, as they believed that if ancient Egyptian hieroglyphs could be interpreted, they might pre-date Biblical accounts of the Flood, when all civilization was supposedly wiped out.

Excavations in Egypt continued throughout the 20th century, (and are still going on), with discoveries such as the ancient tomb in The Valley of the Kings of the boy Pharaoh, Tutankhamen, by Howard Carter and George Herbert in 1922. The discovery of tombs of other ancient Pharaohs proved disappointing, as most of the treasures had been stolen by grave robbers over the millennia, but in the case of Tutankhamen, the tomb was found virtually intact, and the boy Pharaoh's death mask, on display in the Egyptian Museum at Cairo, is one of the most famous and treasured Egyptian artefacts ever to have been discovered.

And Across the Globe

When our early ancestors began their migration out of Africa, they spread north into Mesopotamia, Turkey, Greece, and the rest of Europe. Civilized communities established themselves in the Near East, like the Babylonians, Assyrians, Hittites, Phoenicians, Philistines, etc. Agriculture and sedentary lifestyles were established in south-eastern (modern) Turkey long before 5,000 B.C. Trade was established, especially by the Phoenicians, with their seafaring skills. These people also developed the first alphabet, to replace the complicated, awkward, and unwieldy hieroglyphs and cuneiform scripts.

Eastwards, migration continued to India, and into China. In their wake, these early migrants left behind relics of their stone-age weapons, tools, fishhooks, and sewing needles of bone, and some other artefacts as evidence of their wanderings. The Americas were the last continents to be populated, where cultures like the Mayans, Incas, and Aztecs were established.

Wherever these civilizations emerged, religions developed, with various gods and deities. Religious rituals were performed with animal and, sometimes, human sacrifices, especially in the Americas.

Eventually, the human population occupied every continent on the globe, (except Antarctica), and even remote islands in the Pacific, like Easter Island.

A Brief Summary of Religious Belief

From the earliest history of human civilization, religious belief has always played a dominant role. Indeed, it seems to be closely woven into the very fabric of the human psyche. Wherever you go or whatever society you live in, religion prevails. When you consider that out of the 7 billion humans that populate the Earth, over 2 billion follow the Christian faith, and another 1.5 billion follow the Islamic faith. There are also about 14 million who follow the Jewish faith. All these three stem from the one tree, following the teachings in the Torah, Bible, and Koran. Moses, for example, is revered by the Jews, the Christians, and the Muslims alike. Over the course of time, the religion split three ways—the Christians following the teachings of Christ, and 600 years later the Muslims following the teachings of the prophet, Mohammed, leaving about 14 million Jews following the original teachings of Moses. But basically, all three religions believe in the same things, like the creation of Man in Genesis. Of other religions, Hinduism accounts for 15% of the human population, mainly in India, and Buddhism which started in India but spread to the Far East, about 7%.

No one knows exactly when religious thought began. It probably got started with the worship of the ancient Spiritual Ancestors, which continues this day with some remote cultures in the Pacific Islands and some other more primitive societies.

The earliest evidence of organised religion was the discovery of an ancient temple, Göbekli Tepe, found buried twenty feet under the sand in South-Eastern Turkey where it had lain undiscovered for 11,600 years, predating the Pyramids of Giza by 6,500 years. This ancient stone circle was constructed of perfectly formed T-shaped pillars of rectangular stone, standing 18 feet tall, and carved with the figures of ferocious animals and other creatures. It had been built by a Neolithic people who had only flint tools to work with. Nothing is known of the people who built them, but whoever they were, they obviously worshipped some sort of ancestral spirits of the dead, and the ferocious animals carved on the stone blocks were to act as guardians of the spirit world.

The loss of a close family member or friend must have been a traumatic event even for the ancients to come to terms with. This probably led to the belief that their spirit lived on amongst other ancestral spirits. However, the immediate concern was the disposal of the dead body, and this had to be done rather quickly as a putrefying corpse gave off an offensive smell. In earliest times, the body was disposed of in caves, but later, burials took place, and this probably took the form of a ritual—religious or otherwise. Many ancient burial sites have been found in Europe and Britain, and often trinkets or weapons were buried with the deceased. Each society had its own way of dealing with the dead. Ancient Egyptian Pharaohs were embalmed and placed in their sarcophagi in pyramids or tombs. In Europe, entombment was reserved for the rich and famous in abbeys, churches, and vaults—the less well-off being interned in graves. Zoroastrians, Tibetan-Buddhists, and Red Indians left their dead to be devoured by the birds of the air, while Hindus burnt their corpses, and scattered the ashes in a river, preferably a sacred one.

When gods and other deities were conceived and worshipped, various idols were fashioned. Strangely enough, although the ancient civilizations in the Near East, like the Babylonians, Assyrians, Hittites, Philistines, Phoenicians, etc., lived in such close proximity to each other, religious beliefs were not shared, and each culture had their own specific gods, deities, and religious customs. In other words, religion never 'caught on' from neighbouring cultures, so there was a diversity of different gods and deities worshipped by each society.

The most well known is the ancient Greek religion, and the names of their various gods and goddesses, like Zeus, Apollo, Aphrodite, Ares, Hermes, Poseidon, etc., are familiar names even today. Each of these gods and goddesses represented different aspects or qualities, like light, love, war, communication, and the sea and such, and seemed to be in control of these phenomena. They also interacted with humans, both physically and sexually, and their offspring became demi-gods, like Hercules. Great tales of the exploits of these gods, goddesses, and demi-gods became woven into their ancient Greek mythological writings. Later, the Romans adopted these gods and goddesses, but some of the names were changed, like Aphrodite to Venus, Ares to Mars, Hermes to Mercury, and Poseidon to Neptune, and these are familiar names for some of our planets.

Like the Greek religion, Hinduism followed a similar pattern with their various gods and goddesses interacting with humans, and each deity being in charge of certain aspects or qualities, like Shiva (the destroyer), Lakshmi (wealth), Kali (destruction), Durga (war), and also half-man, half-animal gods like Hanuman (the monkey god) and Ganesh (the elephant god), each representing different attributes.

Buddhism, on the other hand, followed the teachings of Buddha, born a prince, who received divine inspiration while meditating under the Bo tree in Bodh Gaya, and gave up all his wealth to follow divine principles revealed to him. Although all this took place in India, and it flourished there for a while, eventually a resurgent Hinduism prevailed and Buddhism spread north to Tibet and south to Sri Lanka. Also in the 12th century, Muslim invaders destroyed monasteries and monuments in their drive to spread Islam in the region. Thereafter, it spread to the Far East where it is practiced in countries like Burma, China, Korea, and Japan. It took on much of the culture in the different countries where it was practiced, and so has many different forms in the modern day. It is a religion based largely on the philosophy of karma, and rebirth—which is different to the generally held beliefs in re-incarnation, and is a religion that is particularly gentle to all forms of living creatures, as all life is revered.

Unlike the Judeo-Christian-Islamic religion, to which not much reverence is given to animals, most other religions gave veneration to creatures besides humans—the Egyptians thought bulls and cats were sacred; the Hindus revered the cow; the Buddhists embraced all forms of life. Even gods and other deities took on half-human, half-animal forms. In addition, the concept of reincarnation—which was embraced by most other religions—was excluded from most Judeo-Christian-Islamic beliefs.

Furthermore, unlike ancient Egyptian and Tibetan Buddhist texts, which had Books of the Dead, to help the soul through the after world, the Old Testament rarely mentions the afterlife. The texts relate more to God's relationship with man—prophets like Noah, Abraham, and Moses. The Old Testament is mainly concerned with the pact God entered into with Abraham and his descendants, the Children of Israel, to be led to the Promised Land by Moses. As such, it deals more with the material world than the spiritual one. In fact, attempts to communicate with the spirits of the dead were outlawed in the book of Leviticus, where it says, 'I will set my face against the person who turns to mediums and spiritists to prostitute himself by following them, and I will cut him off from his people.' (Leviticus 20:6).

God's laws, delivered through Moses, are mainly concerned with man's obedience to his laws, rather than his spiritual salvation. Various laws were written in the book of Leviticus that deal with dietary and other laws, rituals, and sacrifices—all spelt out for us. For example, it is ordained that man must not eat any animals other than ones that have both the cloven hoof and chew the cud—like cattle, sheep, goats, etc. Eating other animals, like pigs, is forbidden because, although they have the cloven hoof, they do not chew the cud. All these dietary constraints are still followed faithfully by most of the Jewish and Islamic traditions, but were overturned by Jesus, who said it is not what goes into your mouth that defiles you, but what comes out of your mouth, like words of hate, malice, and envy. Also, it is mainly in the New Testament that there is mention of The Kingdom of God and a promise of salvation for the human soul through Jesus.

With the advent of Christianity, a kinder face of God was presented in the form of Jesus. The old concept of 'an eye for an eye and a tooth for a tooth' was replaced with 'turn the other cheek' if you were slapped in the face. Love and forgiveness were the very basic concepts of the Christian faith. It came at a time when the world was still a very barbaric place, and many of the harsher Jewish teachings and traditions of the original Hebrew religion were overturned.

However, the Messiah, whom Christ represented, was never really accepted by the majority of the Jewish population, and instead the message spread to the Gentiles (the non-Jewish populace), some of whom converted, and after Christ's crucifixion and some 49 years later, the apostle Paul spread the message westwards. Paul—a Roman citizen and tax-collector, who had a vision of Christ on his way to Damascus—helped spread the word to Greece and eventually Rome, which finally converted to Christianity under the Roman Emperor, Constantine.

Later, the newly established Roman Catholic Church split into two factions: the Roman Catholic and Eastern Orthodox Churches. In the 16th Century, the Roman Catholic Church again split, and the Church of England was formed. This new church came under the remit of King Henry VIII of England, and its creation followed from the Pope refusing to grant him a divorce from his first wife in order to marry a second. Thereafter, the Church fragmented into several branches of the Christian faith, like the Baptists, Methodists, Pentecostals, Seventh Day Adventists, Unitarians, and The Church of Latter Day Saints (Mormons), mostly established in Europe and England, then spreading to the USA where they could practice their religious faith without undue persecution.

In about 600 A.D., the prophet Mohammed received a vision from God (Allah), and in his vision, the Holy Koran was communicated to him. From thereon, a huge following of the Islamic tradition began, and although centred mostly in the Middle East today, spread to Pakistan and Indonesia to become the most significant religion in those regions.

Meanwhile, the old Hebrew religion still survives mostly in Israel and in pockets all over the world. The Children of Israel, whom Moses led into the Promised Land (formerly Palestine), did not hold on to their God-given country for very long. They were driven into exile by Nebuchadnezzar, king of the Babylonians, who destroyed Jerusalem and the Temple, then after being allowed back, came under Roman occupation and eventually fell victim to warlike neighbours, to be finally driven from the land, and live in communities mostly in Europe and America, never having a homeland for nearly 2,000 years, until the establishment of Israel in 1948 under the auspices of the United Nations. They were always a persecuted people, from the time of their 400-year sojourn in Egypt before being led to their Promised Land by Moses, and then being made unwelcome and expelled in medieval times from various European countries, like England, France, and Spain, to eventually becoming victims to the Nazis in Germany during the Holocaust, where 7 million people perished in the gas chambers of Auschwitz and other Nazi death camps. They are still surrounded by hostile neighbours even to this day.

In the Beginning

Among the many books of the Bible, the first book, Genesis, is one of the most difficult to read, comprehend, and interpret. It can be confusing, contradictory, and ambiguous. It is one of the most controversial too, and is the main cause of disagreement between religious and scientific thought in modern times. Genesis deals mainly with God's relationship with his creation, man, which was not always a happy one. I have attempted to give an account of the book in a very condensed and easy-to-read form, and hope the reader will gain a better understanding of the various characters and God's relationship with them.

The Creation

'In the beginning …' The first three words of arguably the most read book in the world: the Bible. It begins with the creation of Heaven and Earth by a divine creator, God, as he is worshipped by the Judeo-Christian and Islamic religions. It begins quite simply to say that the Earth was *without form and void, and darkness was upon the face of the deep.* Then God created light and darkness, and called them Day and Night. This was on the first day of creation. On the second day, He created the firmament (sky) and the waters above the sky, and on the third day, He created the dry land, plants and trees, and also the seas. On day four, He created the Sun, the Moon, and the stars, and set them in the heavens. On the fifth day, God created fish and all sea creatures, and also the birds of the air.

On the sixth day, He created all land animals and insects, then finally man and woman, and rested on the seventh day, which became the Sabbath.

This order of creation was rather out of step to modern-day creation theories and, to understand the early concept of what was considered the Universe by the ancients, one has to imagine, as they did, that the Earth was a flat disc supported on pillars. On this disc lay the landmasses, which was part of the Middle East, with countries like Iraq, Iran, Syria, and Israel. These were bordered on the north by the 'Abyss of Waters'. A celestial dome called the Firmament in which the Sun and Moon hung, enclosed all this. Then a layer of water, called the 'Upper Waters', divided the Firmament into two sections, the upper being called Heaven where the stars resided. The lower Firmament had portals, through which the upper waters fell down to earth as rain.

Adam and Eve

The creation of the first man, Adam, was fashioned from the dust of the earth, and he was made by God in His own image. In order to provide him with some sort of companionship, the first woman, Eve, was made from one of Adam's ribs.

After the creation of Adam and Eve, God placed them in the Garden of Eden, which lay somewhere between the Tigris and Euphrates rivers in modern day Iraq. In this garden were planted many fruit trees, one of which being the Tree of

Knowledge, and God told Adam that whereas he could eat the fruit of any tree, he must not eat the fruit of the Tree of Knowledge, as otherwise he would die. However, a serpent (Satan in disguise) tempted Eve to eat the fruit and therefore become like gods, knowing the difference between good and evil. She shared this fruit with her husband, Adam, who weakly accepted. As soon as they had done this, they immediately became aware of their nakedness, and covered themselves with fig leaves, which they sewed together as aprons.

God, who was walking about the garden, discovered them, and when he inquired why they had covered themselves, Adam admitted that he had disobeyed God's commandment and eaten the forbidden fruit from the tree, blaming Eve, and she in turn blamed the serpent. God was furious with their utter disobedience and ordered them to leave the Garden of Eden immediately, and placed guards, in the shape of cherubim with flaming swords, to keep Adam and Eve out, as He was afraid that they, now knowing the difference between good and evil, had already become 'as one of us' (gods), and feared that if they also ate of the Tree of Life, which was in the Garden of Eden too, they would live forever.

The above paragraph is rather strange and depicts God strolling in the garden 'in the cool of the day', almost behaving like Zeus—one of the mythical Greek gods, entering into conversation with a human and interacting with him in much the same way. It does not say that Adam actually saw God, but only heard his voice. Also strange, are the words that God utters: '*Behold. The man is become as one of us, to know good and evil; and now, lest he put forth his hand, and take also of the tree of life, and eat, and live for ever.*' This is another Greek-like concept, implying that there were other gods about.

Anyway, Adam and Eve were sent out of the Garden, and Adam had to farm the land, although God cursed him and said all he would reap would be thistles and thorns! Adam and his wife Eve 'knew each other' (the archaic term for the sexual act), and produced two sons, Cain and Abel.

Cain and Abel

The first-born, Cain, farmed the land, and his brother, Abel, was a herdsman, rearing sheep. Both offered gifts to God, but whereas Abel's gifts were acceptable, Cain's were not. Cain was very put out, and in a fit of jealous rage murdered his brother—the first murder on Biblical record. When God inquired of Cain where his brother was, Cain replied that he did not know, and added, '*Am I my brother's keeper?*' This enraged God, as he knew that Cain had slain his brother, and cast him out saying he would forever roam the Earth as a wanderer. This really alarmed Cain, as he greatly feared that without the protection of God he would fall victim to other men who would soon slay him. So, to assuage his fears and protect Cain, God put a mark on him to warn others off, and Cain went to live in the east of Eden in the land of Nod. God also told Cain that whatever he tilled from the ground would not yield any strength. However, Cain did meet and marry a woman, and begat a son, Enoch, and several generations continued from his family line.

Here one has to pause and speculate, because it is not clear *whom* Cain married, for Adam and Eve were the first humans to be created by the hand of God and they produced only two male heirs, so where did Cain's wife come from? This has always been a moot point, which even modern day theologians cannot answer. In addition, since Cain feared being slain by other men, it is clear that there were other humans around, besides Adam, Eve, and Cain. Furthermore, in Genesis Chapter 6, there is some mention of 'the sons of God' marrying 'the daughters of men', who they considered to be very fair and beautiful. One can only presume that the sons of God were the direct descendants of God's divine creation, Adam and his lineage, but the Bible does not make it clear who these daughters of men were, only to say that their offspring were 'Nephilim'—a race of giants. One can only guess at the answer.

Noah and the Ark

Adam and Eve once again 'knew each other' and produced another son to replace Abel, and named him Seth. He again married another of these mysterious women. Many descendants of Adam followed, ending with Noah, famous for building the ark. After Noah reached five hundred years of age, he begat three sons: Shem, Ham, and Japheth.

Again, one has to pause. The descendants of Adam each lived for several hundred years, usually dying when they reached 900-plus years. It is not clear how these 'years' were worked out, but it seems rather incredible that humans could be so long lived as to survive for nearly a thousand years, and still be able to produce children at 500 years of age. However, God was becoming rather fed-up with the proliferation of the species, their longevity, (which he forthwith reduced to 120 years), their violence, corruption, and wickedness, and decided that he would eradicate man from the face of the Earth in a mass extinction: 'the Flood'.

The last of Adam's descendants, Noah, gained favour with God, so he decided to save him and all his family. He instructed Noah to build an ark (a large sort of ship), and take on board with him his wife, his sons and their wives, and a pair of animals of each species, as well as birds and insects of each sex, and gave Noah some time to build the ark according to his directions and collect all the creatures together to put on board before the Earth flooded.

Here we need another pause. ... The *whole* Earth? Of course, the ancient concept of the Earth was not the whole planet as we know it today, but just the region of the Middle East that was in Noah's vicinity. In addition, the collection of creatures could not, of course, have included all the species of animals, birds, and insects we know inhabit the planet today, but just perhaps those that were more familiar in the region, otherwise conditions on the ark would have been very cramped indeed.

So, now having Noah, his family, and collection of creatures safely on board the ark, God sent down the rain to flood the land with waters from the heavens so that every other living thing was drowned. This must have been a very cataclysmic event for all those humans and other creatures still remaining on the Earth, but nonetheless, as indicated in the Bible, they were all wiped out, and Noah and his wife and family were the only ones to survive this catastrophe. The rain continued unabated for 40 days, until everything was 20 feet under water, including the high hills. The waters remained for 150 days. Eventually, day-by-day, the levels decreased and the ark came to rest on the top of Mount Ararat in the seventh month. Noah sent out a dove, and when it returned one day with an olive twig in its beak, Noah realised the waters had abated from the Earth, and God told him it was now safe to leave the ark and settle on dry land, whereupon the grateful Noah built an altar and tendered burnt offerings to God, who—pleased with the sweet savour of burnt flesh—promised that he would never again destroy Man, and sent a rainbow as a pledge to his promise.

The Tower of Babel

Noah lived for another 350 years after the flood, and his kin once again populated the Earth. They migrated to the east and settled on the plain of Babylon, where they built a city with a tall tower to reach to Heaven. When God came down to see their handiwork, He observed that only one language was spoken by all the people, and fearing that if they could build a great city, nothing would be impossible for them, He made them all speak different languages in order to thwart them, and scattered them abroad the face of the Earth, so work on the city ceased. The city was named Babel, because the people could not understand one another. Our word 'babel'—a confusion of words and sounds—derives from this name.

Another observation: It seems that God was always apprehensive that man would become as clever as gods. Having already eaten from the Tree of Knowledge, He prevented them from also eating from the Tree of Life, and limited their lifespan. Here is another example of this anxiety exhibiting itself by confusing their language so they could not communicate with each other. One wonders why this is so.

Abraham

Descended from one of Noah's sons, Shem, Abram was another of God's favourites, and God appeared to Abram in a vision, promising he would make his descendants as many as the number of stars in the heavens. However, Abram was worried as he was already advanced in years and had not yet produced any offspring from his wife Sarai. To assuage his fears, Sarai told him to sleep with her handmaid Hagar, so that he could produce an heir. When Abram followed her advice, and Hagar conceived, she began to look on Abram's wife with contempt, which upset Sarai, so in consultation with Abram, she drove Hagar out of the household. Hagar landed up in the wilderness near a spring of water, and was visited by an angel of the Lord, who told Hagar to return and submit to her mistress, and she would bear a male child whom she should call Ishmael, and it was so.

When Abram reached age 99, the Lord once again appeared to him in a vision and said, 'From henceforth, your name shall no longer be Abram, but Abraham,' and made a covenant with him whereby Abraham and all his male descendants would be circumcised, and that his wife would no longer be known as Sarai but Sarah, and that she would conceive a son whom he should name Isaac. Abraham fell on his face laughing at the thought of a man of nearly a hundred years, fathering a son, but God assured him this would be so, and so it was.

Sodom and Gomorrah

One day, as Abraham sat at the door of his tent, the Lord sent three men (or angels) to visit him, and after they were fed by Abraham and Sarah, the Lord directed Abraham to accompany the men to Sodom as he wanted to know if the sins and wickedness of the people living in the cities of Sodom and Gomorrah were as great as he had heard, and if it were so, he would destroy the cities. Abraham pleaded with God, saying that if there were just fifty righteous people in Sodom, would he spare the city? God replied that if there were only fifty righteous people in the city he would indeed stay his hand. Abraham continued to appeal to the Lord, gradually reducing the figure down to only ten righteous people, and God replied that if there were even ten such people, He would spare Sodom and Gomorrah. But, apparently, there were less than this number of righteous people living in the city. When the angels reached the city gate, Lot, Abraham's nephew, met them and accompanied them to his house where his wife and two daughters lived. However, when the lascivious men of the city spied these angels, who were very fair and beautiful, they lusted after them and surrounded Lot's house, demanding that they should come out so that they could have sex with them. Lot pleaded and even offered his virgin daughters in place of the angels, but they continued with their demands. The angels then caused the men outside to become blind, and led Lot, his wife, and daughters out of the city, and warned them not to look back, otherwise they too would be consumed with what the Lord was about to do. Then God rained fire and brimstone upon Sodom and Gomorrah from the heavens, until the cities were completely destroyed.

This raining down of fire and brimstone is something of a mystery, as there are no active volcanoes spewing out lava in the region that could account for this. To offer some sort of physical explanation, it could, perhaps, have been a meteor or asteroid, breaking up in the atmosphere and raining down fire from the sky.

Lot's wife could not resist having a peek over her shoulder, and she was immediately turned into a pillar of salt. This put Lot's daughters in a quandary, as their father had left no male heir, so they conspired to make their father drunk, and while he was in a drunken stupor, each daughter slept with him in turn, and both became pregnant, and the first daughter bore a son called Moab, who became father of the Moabites, and the younger daughter also bore a son called Ben-ammi who became father of the Ammonites.

This is the first mention of an incestuous relationship recorded in the Bible, and it seems to pass without any sort of criticism or anger on God's part. Of course, in retrospect, the Laws were not yet written.

Abraham and Isaac

When Hagar and Sarah's sons were in their boyhood, Sarah saw Isaac playing with his half-brother Ishmael, the son of Hagar; she became upset, and demanded that Abraham again cast Hagar out of the household. Abraham was reluctant to do this, but God advised him to follow Sarah's wishes, so Hagar and her son were both cast out into the wilderness of Beer-sheba, where they were without food and water. However, God heard Ishmael crying and told Hagar to fear not as he would raise her son, and from his seed would arise a great nation. When Hagar opened her eyes, she saw God had provided a well of water beside them. Later, when her son was grown and became an expert archer, she found an Egyptian wife for him and he and his family dwelt opposite Egypt in the direction of Assyria.

One day, while Isaac was still a child, God wanted to test Abraham's love and obedience, so He directed Abraham to go to the land of Moriah and sacrifice his son as a burnt offering. Abraham followed God's directions, found a suitable place, and built an altar on which to sacrifice his son. However, just as Abraham laid Isaac on a bed of kindling and took out his knife to slay his son, he heard the voice of an angel calling out his name, and saying not to go ahead with the sacrifice, because he had passed God's test, and a ram was provided for the ritual instead.

This demand for a human blood sacrifice, albeit just a test, seems incomprehensible to us in this modern day and age. Of course, Christ himself was referred to as the Lamb of God, and sacrificed himself on the cross for the sins of the world.

Abraham died at the age of 175, and his sons Isaac and Ishmael buried him in a cave with his wife. Isaac married when he was 40 and fathered two twins, Esau and Jacob. When the boys grew, Esau was a skilful hunter and Jacob a quiet man, and probably nomadic, as it says he dwelt in tents. Isaac's favourite son was Esau, but his wife Rebekah, loved Jacob more. One day, while Jacob was boiling pottage, Esau returned from hunting, famished to the point of starvation. He asked Jacob for some, but Jacob demanded that in exchange for this, his brother was to sell him his birth-right, so Esau complied with this blackmail in order to obtain some food.

This case of sibling rivalry is not uncommon in the Bible, and not only did Jacob gain his brother's birth-right by coercion but, later, on their father's deathbed, he also deceived his father, who was now virtually blind, into believing he was his favourite son Esau, and stole his father's blessing too. However, as it turned out, Jacob had a dream of a ladder reaching up to Heaven, and the Lord spoke to him from above, and blessed him and all his descendants, so he became the chosen one, which is rather strange as he behaved in an unscrupulous way by obtaining his brother's birth-right and his father's blessing by extortion and deception.

Joseph and his coat of many colours

Besides his other wives and children, Jacob fathered a son through his wife Rachel, whom he had always loved, and called him Joseph, and he became his favourite son. When Joseph was 17, Jacob (who God now re-named Israel, after he wrestled with, and prevailed against, an angel), made Joseph a coat of many colours. This act of favouritism, on the part of their father, caused jealousy, enmity, and hatred with his brothers. To add to this, Joseph was also a dreamer of dreams, and in his dreams, which he revealed to his brothers, he always dreamt that he had dominion over them. This further angered them, and one day they conspired to kill him, but instead relented and sold him to a passing caravan of Ishmaelites. His brothers stripped Joseph of his robe, dipped it in the blood of a goat, and took it to their father, saying a wild beast had devoured their brother. Understandably, when Jacob was given this news, he was inconsolable, and mourned for his favourite son for many days.

Joseph's captors took him to Egypt, where they sold him to a captain of the Pharaoh's guard, Potiphar. This man took a great liking to Joseph, and was very kind to him, making him his overseer and putting him in charge of all that he owned. However, Joseph—being a handsome man—soon attracted the attentions of Potiphar's wife, who invited him on many occasions to have sex with her. Joseph resisted these advances, and furious at being rebuffed, Potiphar's wife accused Joseph of attempted rape, and his master imprisoned him.

But, the Lord was with Joseph and, even though he was in prison, he prospered under God's love, and was made keeper of all the other prisoners. One day, Pharaoh was angered by two of his household servants, and threw them both into prison, under Joseph's charge. Joseph noticed that they were both troubled, and when he asked them why, they answered that they'd had disturbing dreams, and when they told Joseph of their dreams, he interpreted these for them, which greatly comforted them. Word spread that Joseph had this gift of interpreting dreams, and one day Pharaoh sent for him and told Joseph of a troubling dream, which Joseph interpreted, and warned Pharaoh of an imminent famine that would strike his country, so Pharaoh was able to take preventative measures to avoid this calamity. Pharaoh was very pleased with Joseph, and not only made him a man of great importance in his court, but gave to him in marriage the daughter of one of his high priests.

In later years, Joseph was reunited with his brothers and father when they came to Egypt to buy grain, as there was famine in the land of Canaan where they dwelt. When his father came to know that his son was, after all, alive and well, he was overjoyed. Joseph's brothers repented for the wrong they had done their brother, and so it all ended happily for the family, and they remained in Egypt for the rest of their days.

Out of Egypt

We now come to the second book of the Bible, Exodus. While Genesis deals with many of the early prophets, Adam through to Joseph, Exodus mainly deals with the great prophet Moses. It is thought to have been written between 1580 B.C. and 1215 B.C., though some scholars place the writing of Exodus much later, perhaps as early as the 5th or 6th centuries B.C. This book deals with the relationship between God and Moses, and is set 400 years after the Israelites had settled in Egypt, although there is no archaeological evidence to support this or that they were ever led out of Egypt by Moses in a mass exodus.

When Joseph and all his brethren had died, and all the generations of Jacob had lived in the land of Egypt for 400 years, the children of Israel (the descendants of Jacob) became an oppressed people, as the new Pharaoh feared they had become too many and might join up with their enemies to overthrow the Egyptians. Therefore, the Pharaoh made things hard for the Israelites, placing taskmasters over them and giving them the hardest jobs, like making bricks and mortar, working in the fields, and building storehouses for the Pharaoh.

Pharaoh became so concerned about the ever-growing Hebrew population, that he decreed that henceforth, all new-born male children should be cast into the Nile, but female children be allowed to live.

A male child was born to the daughter of Levi, and seeing that he was a handsome child, she hid him from Pharaoh for three months, then one day, put him in a basket made of bulrushes, and placed it amongst the reeds on the riverbank. Soon, some of the daughters of Pharaoh came to bathe in the river Nile and, seeing the basket and discovering an infant inside, one of the daughters recognised that this was a Hebrew child who would fall victim to her father's commands. She took the child and brought him up as her own in the house of Pharaoh, as she was childless, and named him Moses.

When Moses had grown to adulthood, he witnessed one of his own Hebrew people being mistreated by an Egyptian, so he slew the man, and fearing he would be arrested for this crime, fled from the city to the land of Midian. Here he met the daughter of a sheepherder and married her. She bore him two sons, Gershom and Eliezer. Meanwhile, the Pharaoh died, but the people of Israel were still subjugated by the Egyptians under the next Pharaoh, thought to be Rameses II.

While tending his father-in-law's flock of sheep in the region of Mount Sinai, the mountain of God, the Lord appeared to Moses in the form of a burning bush, and he heard the voice of God calling to him. God told him that he had seen the affliction of Moses's people and directed Moses to take his people out of Egypt to the land of Canaan, a land flowing with milk and honey. Moses felt a bit dubious that he was competent enough to take on this heavy responsibility, but the Lord assured Moses that he was the person He had chosen to carry out this task. Moses then said to the Lord that he was not articulate enough, but God told him that Moses's brother Aaron would speak for him. So, Moses obeyed the voice of God and returned to Egypt with his wife and family to carry out God's will, after his sojourn in the land of Midian for forty years.

On his return to Egypt, Moses and his brother sought audience with Pharaoh and asked him to let their people go. However, Pharaoh was unwilling to listen to this demand and refused. Nevertheless, Moses persisted with his request, and when the Pharaoh stubbornly refused on each occasion, Moses eventually threatened him, saying that if the Pharaoh did not let his people go, he would turn the river Nile into a river of blood. When this happened, and all the water in the city had turned to blood, Pharaoh was still not convinced of the power of the Hebrew god, as his magicians could also perform the same thing.

God commanded Moses to send another plague, this time a multitude of frogs. When this pestilence befell Egypt and the land was full of frogs, Pharaoh relented, and said that if Moses eradicated the frogs from his land, he would indeed let Moses's people go, but once this had happened, Pharaoh went back on his word and still refused to free the Israelites. So God told Moses to send further plagues to afflict the people of Egypt—hordes of flies and gnats, cattle disease, hailstorms to destroy the crops of the fields, dust storms, plagues of locusts, etc., but still Pharaoh refused to release the people of Moses.

Finally, the Lord instructed Moses that each Hebrew household should slaughter a lamb and daub some of the blood on the doorposts and lintels of their houses. Then they should feast on the lambs that night and eat this with unleavened bread and bitter herbs, for the Lord would pass over the land and send a destroyer to kill the firstborn son of every household in the land that was not protected by the blood of the lamb; the houses that were, the Lord would pass-over.

At midnight, the Lord passed over the land and smote the first-born son of every household that did not have the blood of the lamb on its doorposts and lintels, and this included the house of Pharaoh, whose first-born son fell victim to the destroyer. This night became known as the Passover, and is celebrated in every Jewish household to this day.

With this final pestilence, the Pharaoh finally became convinced of the power of the Hebrew god, and released the Israelites from bondage, and they left the city of Rameses with all their goods and chattels, including their flocks and herds, and Moses led them out from the land of Egypt in the direction of the Red Sea.

There is some debate as to whether this was, in fact, the Red Sea, and theories exist that this was a confusion in translation between the words 'red' and 'reed', and it was to the Sea of Reeds, that Moses took his people. This sea of reeds was a marshy land that lay somewhere between the Red Sea and the Mediterranean. Whatever, they did not follow the usual route—the way of the land of the Philistines (through modern-day Suez), although that was nearer, as there was a war in this region and the followers of Moses might be hindered, and instead might decide to return to the land of Egypt. To guide and protect them, God sent a pillar of cloud to lead them through the day, and a pillar of fire to lead them through the night.

After the release of the Israelites from the land, Pharaoh realised his folly in letting go of these people, who were a useful labour force, so he sent an army with horses and chariots to follow and capture them, and bring them back to Egypt.

At this point, the children of Israel doubted Moses's leadership, and protested that Moses had brought them out into the wilderness to die, and it would be better if they returned to Egypt and served the Egyptians again rather than be buried in the sand.

One can understand their plight, for they were trapped between the sea and the Pharaoh's army. However, God placed the pillar of cloud between the Israelites and the Pharaoh's army to protect them from attack. Then the Lord instructed Moses to raise his rod and part the waters of the sea to let the people through dry land, and when Moses obeyed and the waters parted, the people were able to pass safely to the other bank. God then bid Moses to lower his hand and cause the sea to come crashing back to drown Pharaoh's army, whom He had allowed to follow close on the heels of the Israelites.

Then Moses led Israel onward from the sea into the wilderness. Here, they found little water, and what bit they did find proved undrinkable. Eventually, they found an oasis with springs and palm trees, and they tarried a while. However, when Moses led them on, the people again began to murmur their discontent, and said they were better off in Egypt where they had at least food to eat and water to drink, whereas Moses and Aaron had led them into a land where there was neither. The Lord, hearing their discontent, sent manna from Heaven to rain down from the sky and ordered the people to gather this up and eat it. (This they ate and survived on for 40 years until they came to more habitable land on the borders of Canaan.) However, the children of Israel were still discontented, and in their recriminations, they blamed Moses for bringing them out of the land of Egypt into a barren and waterless wilderness. However, God instructed Moses to take his rod and strike a rock, and when he followed God's instruction, a spring of water came from the rock, so that the people's thirst was quenched.

Three months after leaving Egypt, they came to the wilderness of Sinai and camped before the mountain. Then, as the mountain was obscured by cloud, God summoned Moses to the top of Mount Sinai. Here, he instructed Moses to deliver Ten Commandments to the people. These were: not to worship any other gods; not to worship any graven image; not to take the name of God in vain; to keep the Sabbath and make it holy; to honour thy father and mother; not to kill; not to commit adultery; not to steal; not to bear false witness against your neighbour; not to covet your neighbour's house, nor his wife, or anything that was his.

After Moses had spent forty days and forty nights on Mount Sinai, he came down from the mountain, and carried with him two tablets of stone, on which God had inscribed His commandments.

Of course, it is perfectly feasible that it was Moses himself who inscribed the two stone tablets, as he was educated enough to do this and also had sufficient time on the mountain. Had he been illiterate like most of his followers, gone up to the mountain and returned a day or so later with the inscribed tablets, it would have been far more believable that it was the finger of God that had written the Ten Commandments on the stone tablets. There is also some debate amongst scholars as to the location of the Biblical holy mountain where Moses received the Ten Commandments.

Meanwhile, the Israelites below the mountain, in the absence of their leader—and under the directions of his brother Aaron, who had been left in charge—melted down all their gold jewellery and made a golden calf, which they now worshipped. Moses's utter fury with his people can only be imagined, and he cast the two tablets of stone down on a rock and broke them. He gathered around him the sons of Levi (his tribe) and sent them amongst the people with swords, and they slew 3000 men, women, and children who had sinned against the Lord.

It is quite inconceivable to us today, to understand how Moses could be responsible for the genocide of so many of his own people, whom he had brought out of Egypt under God's direct commandment, especially since he had received God's new commandment: 'Thou shalt not kill'. In fact, he was the first one to break this commandment!

Nevertheless, God's relationship with Moses was a very special one, and he spoke to him 'face to face' as a man speaks to his friend (although Moses never saw the face of God at any time). As the Bible says, there never was another prophet who had such a close relationship with God, or was so invested with the power of the Lord.

While on Mount Sinai, God also gave Moses very detailed and precise instructions for building The Ark of The Covenant, a highly decorated and elaborate casket made of gold, to house the two tablets of stone, containing God's Ten Commandments, which he re-made to replace the ones Moses had broken. When Moses came down from Mount Sinai again, the skin of his face shone with a holy light, which made the people fearful of approaching him. (Of course, their fear could also have stemmed from the fact he had ordered to be killed so many of their comrades.) Moses also instructed the children of Israel to build a tabernacle, a portable tent-like structure, surrounded by a curtain, to house the Ark of the Covenant, which they constructed under his supervision. This sacred site symbolised God's presence amongst the people, and was to be erected wherever they travelled.

The Bible continues with other books about Moses, like Leviticus, Numbers, and Deuteronomy, which tells of the travels of the Israelites in the wilderness to finally reach the Promised Land. The story ends with the death of Moses, who God never allowed to enter into the Promised Land. He died at the age of 120, but 'his eye was not dim, nor his natural force abated'. He was buried in the valley of the land of Moab. His follower, Joshua—the son of Nun—who was full of the spirit of the Lord, was placed in charge of the people and finally led them into the Promised Land.

The Messiah

As far back as the book of Isaiah in the Old Testament, it was prophesised that a Messiah—the Anointed One—would be sent as a redeemer to free the people (the Israelites) from their sins. To the Christian converts, this was in the shape of Jesus of Nazareth, but most of the Jews of the day never accepted that Jesus represented the Messiah.

Very little is known about the early life of Jesus, except in accounts of his birth given in the Gospels of Matthew and Luke, though they are largely different in detail. It is recounted that he was born during the reign of Herod the Great and that his birth was by divine conception of the Virgin Mary. The story of the Nativity is a well-known one. Mary was given in marriage to Joseph, several years her senior, whilst carrying the baby Jesus, and it was during their travels that she gave birth to her baby boy in a manger in the town of Bethlehem. The only account of Jesus's childhood was when he was a boy of about 12 years and the priests at the Temple in Jerusalem were astonished at his religious knowledge. Apart from that, nothing is known of his earlier life until his ministry began at about age 30.

He had a humble family, and his father is said to have been a carpenter. After Jesus's birth, his mother Mary and earthly father Joseph had four other sons: James, Joses, Judas, and Simon, but little is mentioned about them—except for James, who played an important role in the Apostolic Age and established a Judeo-Christian church after his brother Jesus was crucified.

How Jesus spent his early youth is unknown. Did he remain with his family in Nazareth and become a carpenter, or did he travel to other lands? There is some speculation that he might have joined a caravan and travelled the Silk Road to Tibet, as it is claimed that there were some ancient Tibetan writings revealed to a War Correspondent, Nicolas Notovitch, in 1887, that there was a very righteous man from the West who once resided with the monks in a monastery in Tibet, where he acquired some of his philosophies of kindness and gentleness, and humility and compassion, that Buddhism teaches. As romantic as this story sounds, it has largely been discredited, mainly by Wilhelm Schneemelcher who stated that Notovich's accounts were fabrications, as no one has even had a glimpse at the manuscripts Notovitch claims to have had.

Whatever, his ministry began with his baptism by John the Baptist, when it is said the spirit of God entered into him. He then went into self-exile in the wilderness for 40 days and had encounters with the Devil who tried to tempt him into turning stones into bread and offering him great wealth and power. When he resisted these temptations, and came out of the wilderness, he recruited 12 Apostles, who accompanied him in his mission.

During his three-year ministry, he preached messages of love, kindness, forgiveness, and humility, which were way ahead of their time in the barbaric society in which he lived. He performed many miracles, like healing the sick and giving the blind sight, and was not even above small acts of kindness and consideration, such as changing water into wine at a wedding party to save the host embarrassment when the wine had run out. He even fed the multitude he preached to by performing a miracle to turn a few measly loaves and fishes into abundance so all could be fed. He also overturned some of the harsher and orthodox Jewish laws by intervening in the stoning of a prostitute by saying, 'You who is without sin cast the first stone.' His main theme was one of repentance and the relinquishing of worldly goods. As he himself said, he had not even a pillow to lay his head on.

However, by his acts and preaching, he upset the Jewish priests and hierarchy who accused him of blasphemy, so his message never got through to his own people, steeped in their orthodox traditions, and instead spread to the Gentiles (the non-Jewish populace) who accepted the values of his teachings more readily.

Eventually, his claims to divinity—being one with the Father, and his criticisms of the Scribes and Pharisees for their hypocrisy—upset the Jewish priesthood. So when Jesus entered Jerusalem, and commemorated the Jewish Passover at a meeting with his disciples known as The Last Supper, one of his disciples betrayed him (Judas Iscariot), and he was arrested. The Jewish hierarchy then persuaded the Roman Governor, Pontius Pilate, to try him as a blasphemer and have him executed. Reluctant to do this, the governor washed his hands saying that he could find no fault with the man, and referred him back to Herod Antipas, the puppet king of Israel. When found guilty, Jesus was scourged and sent for crucifixion under Roman law.

Crucifixion entailed nailing the victim to a crude wooden cross by his hands and feet, and leaving him to die in the hot sun. In this position, the unfortunate would usually drown in his own bodily fluids as his lungs filled with water. Sometimes, the executioners would break the legs of the victim to hasten his death.

So, thus was Christ crucified on a Friday, together with two other criminals at Golgotha—the Place of the Skull—his mother Mary and Mary Magdalene being witnesses, as also the Apostle John, whom Jesus loved. In his dying moments, he forgave one of the other criminals being crucified with him, saying, 'Today, you will be with me in Paradise.' He also forgave those who crucified him, saying, 'Father, forgive them, for they know not what they do.' The execution took about 6 hours, and just after the final moments, when Jesus cried out, 'My God, My God. Why hast thou forsaken me?' he 'gave up the ghost'. A Roman centurion speared him in the side, but spared him having his legs broken, as they believed him already dead.

According to Christian tradition, Jesus was always referred to as the sacrificial 'Lamb of God'. In other words, all the sins of the world were to be laid upon Him so that, by his death and resurrection, forgiveness would be given to all who believed in

Him. 'He died to save us all,' is the oft-repeated call of all devout Christians.

When Jesus's body was taken down from the cross by Joseph of Arimathea, (who had approached Pilate for custody of the body), it was placed in a new tomb that had been hewn into a rock, as it was the Jewish tradition that dead bodies were not left out in the open after sunset. A large boulder sealed the entrance to the tomb, and a guard stood outside. The crucifixion was carried out on a Friday, and on the following Sunday some women (traditionally thought to be Jesus's mother Mary and Mary Magdalene amongst them) arrived at the tomb to anoint Jesus's body with myrrh and precious oils, but when they rolled back the boulder at the entrance, they found the tomb empty, except for the linen that had been used to wrap Jesus's body, and an angel appeared to tell them that he had 'arisen' from the dead.

This Resurrection of Jesus is the very foundation of Christian belief. It meant that Jesus had not died on the cross but had *physically* arisen from the dead. From thereon he was referred to as 'The Living Christ'. Later, he appeared to his disciples and they examined his wounds, before he ascended into Heaven.

But, just suppose Jesus had not actually died on the cross. Suppose those initially attending his body had found him to have simply been unconscious or in a coma, and they had been able to revive and spirit him away. If so, he would surely have been hidden safely until he appeared to his disciples later. Thus he would have had to spend the rest of his life in hiding, probably leaving the country. There are legends of a very holy man from the West having lived and eventually died in Kashmir, India. Conspiracy theories also abound with books like *The Da Vinci Code* and *The Holy Blood and the Holy Grail*, where it is supposed that Jesus and Mary Magdalene had a child together, and that their bloodline continues to this day as the Holy Grail.

Because the historic life of Jesus is shrouded in mystery, it is open to speculation by scholars and religious theologians. Who was this mysterious and righteous man? Was he the Messiah? Was he just a learned and religious teacher? Was he God incarnate? Whatever your religious beliefs, he is certainly a revered prophet by all Muslims—Sunnis and Shiahs alike, and to most others of no particular religious persuasion, as a 'Gandhian' figure, whose message was only of love for one's fellow men, forgiveness, goodness, and mercy.

The Spread of Christianity

The basis of all Christian belief is founded on the four Canonical Gospels of The New Testament: Matthew, Mark, Luke, and John, as also the letters (Epistles) of the Apostle Paul. Paul's letters were the first writings in the New Testament, and are usually dated from circa 49 to around 63 A.D; however, most contemporary scholars agree that the earliest of the Gospels is the Gospel of St. Mark, written between 66 and 74 A.D. It opens not with the Nativity story, but with Jesus's baptism by John the Baptist, whereas both the Gospels of Matthew and Luke give an account of Jesus's birth, although they differ in detail. The last Gospel of St. John does not mention the Nativity story at all, and is the most recent of all the Gospels, being written near the beginning of the first century A.D. It is largely agreed by religious scholars that the Gospel of Mark was used as a source for the Gospels of Matthew and Luke, while John is rather different from the other three, which are termed 'Synoptic' Gospels, as they are mostly in agreement with each other. Matthew and Luke have the most in common, and both mention the Lord's Prayer; however, this is not contained in either Mark or John. These four Canonical Gospels are woven into one story about the life of Jesus and his ministry, and is the common theme in children's books and epic Hollywood films.

Apart from the four Canonical Gospels, which were accepted for inclusion into the Bible, there are many other gospels like the Gospel of Thomas, the Gospel of Peter, the

Gospel of Judas, the Gospel of James, the Gospel of Philip, and the Gospel of Mary Magdalene. These other gospels, some of which were unearthed at Nag Hammadi (Egypt) as recently as the last century, were considered heretical by the Church and not given any credence. Some of these were considered to be Gnostic writings.

The Gnostics were an early religious pseudo-Christian sect that believed that salvation lay not in worshipping the risen Christ but in psychic souls who had to free themselves from the material world by revelation and enlightenment. In the Gospel of Judas, for example, he claims that Jesus had spoken to him of secret things, and that he acted in obedience to Jesus's request to betray him, so that by his death, his spirit could be released from his physical body. This Gospel of Judas, thought to be dated about A.D. 230, was found in the 1970s near Beni Masar (Egypt) as a leather-bound papyrus document. On the other hand, the Gospel of Thomas (attributed to Thomas Didymus—the 'doubting' Thomas), gives no details of the life of Jesus or his ministry, but focuses mainly on the sayings of Jesus. It does not even mention his crucifixion or resurrection.

Following Christ's crucifixion, at least three of his apostles, St. Peter, St. James (Jesus's brother), and St. John, established early Judeo-Christian churches, where the teachings of Jesus were preached orally to the converts, Jewish and Gentile, generally thought to be in Aramaic, because the Gospels, as we know them, had not yet been written. Thus, early Christianity began in quite a small way.

It was only after the conversion of the apostle, St. Paul, who experienced a vision of the resurrected Jesus while travelling to Damascus, that the message of Christianity really began to spread. Paul (previously named Saul) was a Jew, a Roman citizen, and a native of Tarsus, the capital city in the Roman province of Cilicia. By profession, he was a tax collector, and before his conversion, vigorously persecuted the converts of early Christianity. In his vision, Jesus appeared to him in a bright light, which temporarily blinded him, and he heard a voice saying, 'Saul! Saul! Why are you persecuting me?' This revelation was a life-changing experience for Paul (who thereon changed his name from Saul to Paul), and he devoted the rest of his life to spreading the message of Christianity, travelling far and wide, and eventually to Rome itself. He wrote many epistles (letters), included in the New Testament, which are considered to be the earliest Christian writings in the Bible, pre-dating the Gospels by several decades.

In pagan Rome, under the Roman emperor Nero, early converts to Christianity were terribly persecuted, and literally thrown to the lions in the arenas for the entertainment of the local citizens. They had to practise their newly found religion in secret, and were generally considered 'enemies of the state'. Yet they stoically endured all the persecution and tortures metered out to them, and determinedly hung on to their newly acquired faith. Even apostles like St. Peter became martyrs to their faith under the heel of the Roman sandal!

This persecution endured for almost 300 years, until the Emperor of Rome, Constantine, converted to Christianity, and it became the official Roman religion. From thereon, it spread to all parts of the Roman Empire, and Constantinople (modern day Istanbul) became capital of the Byzantine Roman Empire.

Because there was a lot of argument, dissension, and division in religious belief at the time, Emperor Constantine intervened, and convened the First Council of Nicaea in A.D. 325. About 300 religious leaders from all parts of the Empire were invited to attend this convention to obtain consensus and settle certain Christological issues, such as the establishment of the true nature of Christ as Son of God to God the Father, and the Nicaean Creed was compiled to establish what was the basis of Christian belief. It is still recited at Holy Communion services in some churches, like the Church of England, and forms part of the indoctrination procedure for candidates to the Confirmation ritual that takes place for those re-affirming their Baptismal vows taken by their God Parents.

The Council of Nicaea was also given the task of examining religious texts and separating 'the wheat from the chaff'. In other words, incorporating into the Bible certain scriptures, which were thought to be divinely inspired, and throwing out those whose origins were questionable, or considered heretical.

However, religious differences still persisted, and eventually the Eastern Orthodox Church split off from the Church of Rome, and further divisions took place in later centuries with the establishment of the Lutheran Church, and the Church of England under King Henry VIII. Further fragmentations continued through the centuries, and today there is a plethora of various churches, each with their own philosophy, theology, and doctrine. Most still believe in the fundamentals like Jesus being the Son of God, his Virgin Birth, and the Crucifixion and Resurrection, and the differences are mainly in religious dogma. For instance, the Baptists believe in adult baptism; the Seventh Day Adventists believe the Sabbath to be on a Saturday and not Sunday; the Unitarians do not believe in The Trinity—that is God the Father, God the Son, and God the Holy Ghost all being one entity.

In all this confusion, one can ask oneself how well has the original message of Jesus's teachings survived? His message was one of love for God and love for one's neighbour, repentance, and forgiveness. Yet in his name the most terrible atrocities have been committed through the centuries by the established Church—the burning of heretics, witches, and such; the terrible tortures inflicted on those who differed in their thoughts or ideas during the Spanish Inquisition. Even William Tyndale, who dared to make an English translation of the Bible in 1535 from the Greek and Hebrew texts, was strangled and burnt at the stake as a heretic for his efforts!

In England, after the Reformation, persecution and terrible acts of torture and cruelty were carried out by both the Protestants towards the Roman Catholics, and the Roman Catholics towards the Protestants, depending on who was in power at the time. Was this what Jesus wanted? I am sure it is not, and sadly it seems that his message of peace, love, and forgiveness was forgotten or corrupted, and all in the name of the established Church.

Happily today, in this 'sinful world' as some devout people might describe it, we have turned into a far kinder society, with greater tolerance towards one another. With the steady demise of the influence and power of the Church in our everyday lives and experience, one is allowed freedom of thought and expression. However, religious fundamentalism still exists in some extreme religious groups, cults, and sects; and acts of murder, execution, and suicide still persist to this day—all carried out in the name of an apparently vengeful God.

Angels and Demons

Throughout the Bible there are many references to angels. It must be considered that the Judeo-Christian-Islamic God at the time of the Creation did not reside on his own in Heaven, but was surrounded by other deities like angels, cherubim, and seraphim, which he also created. The last two are usually thought to be naked winged babies—the cherubs depicted in later Renaissance paintings—but actually, when God commanded Adam and Eve out of the Garden of Eden, he placed cherubim with flaming swords to prevent Adam and Eve from entering the Garden again, so these seem very unlikely candidates for winged infants! They are probably the first mention of other beings, besides Adam and Eve, existing at that time. In earlier Christian artistic depictions, these cherubim are portrayed as quite ferocious creatures with faces of a lion, ox, eagle, and man, peering out from the center of an array of four wings.

In early Gnostic writings, they believed that there were lesser gods, some of whom were not quite so benign. This might explain God's reference to 'become one of us' when Adam and Eve were tempted to eat of the fruit of the Tree of Knowledge.

Among the several references to angels, it states in the Bible that Lucifer (Satan) was himself created by God as a cherub, the most powerful of all angelic beings. He was once loved by God, but his pride and vanity caused him to fall from God's grace. He then rebelled against God in a power struggle in Heaven, and became the epitome of evil. As a fallen angel, he was expelled to Earth where the struggle continued as the war between God and Devil ('good and evil'). It was Satan, in the form of a serpent, who tempted God's new creation, Man, to partake of the Forbidden Fruit (popularly but wrongly thought to be an apple). When he, at the instigation of Eve, obeyed God's arch-enemy, God seemed to lose his faith in his creation, and according to the Bible, this resulted in 'original sin' which we are all still paying for to this day.

Satan took with him to Earth one-third of angels who rebelled against God. Perhaps these beings mated with each other (there is nothing to say that they were asexual) and their female progeny became 'the daughters of men', one of which Cain married. This is purely conjecture, but it would explain how these daughters of men came about, and how their offspring became a race of giants (Nephilim).

All this sounds a bit like a Star Wars epic—a battle of the forces of good against evil. Where did all this take place? Is Heaven an extra-terrestrial civilization that exists somewhere in this vast and unending Cosmos? In the Bible, Heaven is always referred to as the Kingdom of God, where He presides. Are angels and devils the population of two opposing civilizations in constant conflict? Are we the dummies in the middle of it all?

Accounts of angels appear throughout the Bible. The instance of an angel intervening in the sacrifice of Isaac; the wrestling of an angel with Jacob; the visitation of three angels to Abraham when he conducted them to Sodom; the appearance of the Angel Gabriel announcing to Mary that she would give birth to a baby boy; an angel heralding Christ's birth to the shepherds; the appearance of an angel at Christ's empty tomb, saying he had arisen. These are just some references to angels contained in both the Old and New Testaments.

However, what are these heavenly beings? In all paintings and statues, they are depicted as having wings giving them the ability to fly. However, nowhere in the Bible does it say that these are winged creatures. It simply says they ascended, descended, or appeared, which could mean some form of levitation. Nonetheless, whatever they were, they were certainly easily identifiable as being non-human. Additionally, they were apparently very physical beings and not something insubstantial. After all, they physically wrestled with Jacob. They also physically ate and drank when Abraham offered them refreshment in his tent in the desert. They also seemed to be of extreme beauty, which led the licentious men of Sodom to lust after them. The Angel Gabriel is mentioned often in the Bible as being God's special messenger.

Demons, on the other hand, are malevolent beings thought to dwell in Hell, though coming to Earth from time to time to taunt and torment us. They are believed to be followers of Satan as the fallen angels were. They are thought to have the ability to enter into ourselves and take possession of our souls, and among many of Jesus's miracles was the casting out of devils, which we term 'exorcism' today, and which has been performed by priests of many cultures and religions.

Among these entities are djinns—which are spiritual creatures mentioned in the Koran and other Islamic texts. To us, in the Western world, they are often referred to as 'genies', such as the one Aladdin found in the lamp. In Islamic cultures, djinns, angels, and humans make up the three sapient creations of God. Whereas they believe God created Adam from dust, He created the djinn from fire. They have the ability to interact with us humans, and like us, can be either good or evil. They can take on other forms like vultures, snakes, and tall men in white garb. They can also inhabit inanimate objects like rocks and stones, and indeed lamps!

In his apocalyptical Gospel, Revelation, written in about A.D. 95 or thereabouts, Saint John the Divine reveals his vision of a battle of good against evil in the Final Days of Earth: the Armageddon. In this last book of the New Testament, he writes about The Beast with the number 666. This has been popularised in many books and is used as themes for films like *The Omen* and *Rosemary's Baby*, when Satan seeks to gain control of the world by planting his seed on Earth as the Antichrist. In his visions, St. John describes demons such as Scorpion-tailed Locusts, the Whore of Babylon (the mother of all prostitutes and abominations of the Earth riding upon the Seven-headed Beast), the Beast or Antichrist, and the Four Horsemen of the Apocalypse—representing Pestilence, War, Famine, and Death. In his vision, he also sees many trumpet-bearing Angels, representing the forces of good, who battle with the forces of evil. But good triumphs over evil in the end, and those with the 'Seal of the Lamb' on their foreheads survive the Armageddon, which culminates in the Second Coming of Jesus Christ.

When this happens, the Day of Judgment will take place. In Christian theology, Judgment Day is the final eternal judgment by God of every nation on Earth. Mention of this is found in all four Canonical Gospels, particularly in the Gospel of Matthew. In this theology, all human souls would be re-joined, or resurrected with their bodies. Christ would then stand in judgment and separate the 'sheep from the goats' (the good from the bad). The righteous would ascend into Heaven, and the wicked would be thrown into the fires of Hell, where there would be 'wailing and gnashing of teeth'. Therefore, in this theology, it means that when we die, we do not immediately go to Heaven or Hell, but our souls go to an intermediate place until they are judged. In the Roman Catholic doctrine, this intermediate place is called Purgatory.

In the early days after the Crucifixion of Christ, it was thought that this Second Coming of Christ was imminent, and phrases like 'The day of the Lord is nigh,' were oft repeated to remind us to repent of our sins and face the Lord. However, more than 2000 years have passed, and though even today the 'end of days' is often predicted and prophesised, thankfully nothing so far has happened. However, this apocalyptic event is often looked forward to by those of a religious ilk, and the Second Coming of Christ to herald it all is still the theme of many religious preachings.

Chariots of Fire

According to ancient alien theorists, accounts of gods and deities, depicted in various religious mythologies, are thought to be ancient extra-terrestrial visitors to our planet in the dim and distant past. These 'aliens' that supposedly came down to Earth, made contact with us humans and influenced the development of human cultures, religions, and technologies. Not only did these ancient visitors have close encounters with humans, but interacted sexually to produce offspring with special qualities, to help development of the human species. These theorists suggest that because of the special powers of such beings, they were looked up to and revered as gods by ancient cultures like the Greeks.

The Greeks certainly had their array of gods and goddesses, all endowed with special powers or qualities. Unlike Christian doctrine, their gods took both male and female form and led active sexual lives, mating both with each other and with humans, to produce offspring like Heracles (the equivalent for the Roman Hercules), who was the son of the Greek god Zeus; and the mortal, Alcmene, who was famous for his great strength and numerous adventures in Greek mythology.

All these Greek gods had special qualities and ruled over various terrestrial territories. For example:

Zeus—The most powerful king and father of all the other gods, who ruled over the sky and fired thunderbolts at the unsuspecting. According to *The Iliad*, he is father of the female goddess of beauty—Aphrodite (Venus)—and is well known for his erotic escapades, which resulted in many godly and heroic offspring, like Athena (Minerva), Apollo, Artemis (Diana), Hermes (Mercury), Heracles (Hercules), and even the famous deity Helen of Troy, whose abduction by Paris caused the Trojan War. His Roman name was Jupiter, the king of the planets, and as we know, the largest planet in our Solar System is named after him.

Apollo—Recognised as the god of light and the Sun. He had many female lovers and fathered many children. He also had many male lovers, and in today's society would be described as bi-sexual. He is often identified with Helios, a handsome god associated with the Sun, who drove a golden chariot, drawn by fiery horses, across the sky each day.

Poseidon—Perhaps better recognised by his Roman name Neptune, is the God of the Sea, his domain being the ocean, but according to Plato, his chosen domain was the lost island of Atlantis. He is depicted as an older male with curly hair and carrying a trident. He is thought to be the 'earth shaker' and is responsible for earthquakes. The last planet in our Solar System is named after him.

Hermes—Also known by his Roman name of Mercury. He is the god of transitions and boundaries, freely moving between the worlds of the mortal and the divine. He is depicted as a young man wearing a helmet with wings, and carries a winged staff of two intertwined serpents. He is an emissary and messenger of the gods. Our closest planet to the Sun, Mercury, is named after him due to its quick movements around the Sun.

Hades—He is the Greek god of the underworld, and his Roman name is Pluto. He is in charge of the world of the dead. In Christian theologies, this is thought to be Hell. He is often depicted with his three-headed dog, Cerberus. The planetoid Pluto at the edge of the Solar System is named after him, and not the Disney dog!

Athena—She is the goddess of wisdom, courage, inspiration, law and justice, and things like mathematics, the arts, crafts, and skills. Her Roman name is Minerva. The Greek city of Athens, where the Parthenon on the Acropolis is founded, was named after her.

Artemis—Or her Roman equivalent Diana, is the goddess of hunting, wild animals, childbirth, and virginity. She is the twin sister of Apollo. She is often depicted as carrying a bow and arrows. She is also considered the protector of young girls, bringing and relieving diseases in women, and aiding childbirth. So she is very much a goddess for animals and women.

Ares—His Roman name is Mars and he is the god of war. He represents violence, death, and destruction. His two horses, Fear and Terror, drew his battle chariot. He wasn't very well regarded in Greek mythology, and his father, Zeus, once told him he was the most hateful of all his sons. He was more revered by the Romans and they gave him more distinction than the Greeks. He had many lovers, including the goddess of beauty, Aphrodite (Venus). Mars, our neighbouring red planet representing the blood of war, is named after him.

Aphrodite—The goddess of beauty and love, also known by her Roman equivalent, Venus. According to Homer, she was the daughter of Zeus and Dione. She had many lovers, both gods and men, and was lover and additionally surrogate mother to Adonis, a very handsome youth. Our brightest planet, Venus, is named after her.

The mere mention of gods, like Apollo riding in a fiery chariot through the sky, has inspired ancient-alien theorists to think of them as some sort of fiery spacecraft. There is also mention of the prophet Elijah ascending into Heaven in a fiery chariot. He is credited with bringing down fire from the sky. In a later chapter of the New Testament, he is transfigured (physically changed) with Christ together with Moses, in a bright and blinding light, and ancient-alien theorists interpret this as a hologram from some sort of spacecraft hovering above.

It is speculated by ancient-alien theorists that these gods, or visitors to our planet in the past, had some influence on our genetic makeup and our culture. If so, how far back does this go? Did these god-like figures really have any influence on the creation of modern man? Whatever, there is certainly a great difference between Man and his closest relative, the chimpanzee. No missing link between the two species has ever been found, and even Darwin's theory of evolution does not fully explain how Man evolved from animals, saying only that, 'Light will be thrown on the origin of man and his history,' presumably in the future.

The fact that many people believe that not a single shred of evidence has been left behind by these supposed ancient aliens is making the argument of these 'visitors' to our planet very insubstantial. However, there are some unexplained mysteries regarding the technologies our ancient ancestors possessed in undertaking such projects as the Nascar Lines in Peru—those hundreds of ancient drawings on the ground of humming birds, spiders, monkeys, and fish—which can only be viewed from an aircraft. Or the massive terraced walls at Saksaywarman where stone blocks, weighing some 50 to 100 tons, are so perfectly manoeuvred and fitted into place that the seams seem to be almost moulded together, as not even a sheet of paper can be inserted between them. One wonders if they had some help from above? Speculation will continue and, no doubt, some explanation will emerge during the course of time.

Meanwhile, the question of UFOs will continue to be investigated, and one day some substantial evidence may be found, as to whether visitations of extra-terrestrial beings to our planet are authentic. There are certainly quite credible accounts of these sightings by very reliable people, who have seen strange objects in the sky like flying saucers and such. There are also accounts of close encounters from people who think they might have been abducted and experimented upon by alien beings. Whether these accounts are credible or not is a matter of debate. It is certainly not impossible that somewhere in this vast cosmos intelligent beings have found some means of travelling through the infinity of space and time to reach us, and are still hovering around our planet and keeping us under surveillance. Whatever the case, if these aliens exist they have been clever in concealing themselves and not leaving behind indisputable evidence of their visitations. However, with the profusion of hand-held video cameras and mobile phone devices about, it is probable that some reliable images will be taken, and in time to come this mystery may someday unravel. Until then, we will have to leave the question in the realms of science fiction writers.

Heroes, Legends, and Myths

Throughout the history of literature, there have been various myths and legends about heroes and super-heroes. Beginning with the ancient Greeks, epic tales were recounted in Homer's Iliad and Odyssey. These take the forms of poems and are the oldest works of Western literature.

Ulysses—The Odyssey centres on the Greek hero, Odysseus, better known by his Roman name, Ulysses. After the fall of Troy, it takes Ulysses ten years to reach Ithaca, an island located in the Ionian Sea near Greece. During this time, he was assumed to have died. The story recounts his adventures, such as his capture by Cyclops, a giant with one eye in the middle of his forehead, whom he slays by driving a wooden stake through this eye. He also encounters the Sirens, beautiful women-creatures who lure unsuspecting sailors with their enchanting music and voices, to wreck their boats on the rocks.

Hercules—Another divine Greek hero, who was a demi-god, being the son of the Greek god, Zeus, was Hercules. This super-hero possessed great strength and had many adventures, like the slaying of the Nemean Lion, a vicious beast with sharp, armour-piercing claws. He also slew the Hydra, a nine-headed serpent-like monster, which could immediately grow another head if one was cut off. Furthermore, he captured the Golden Hind, an enormous deer with golden antlers and hooves of bronze or brass. These adventures were part of his 'Twelve Labours', which he was entrusted to fulfil.

Samson—The Bible, too, has its heroes, and among the most prominent is Samson, one of the Old Testament Judges, who was in possession of super-human strength, and who battled against the Philistines, slaying several of them using only the jaw-bone of an ass. However, his vulnerability lay in his mane of long hair, which—as a Nazarite—he was not permitted to shave or cut. If this were done, he would lose his strength and become as powerless as other men. However, he was seduced by Delilah, who was bribed by the Philistines to find out the secret of his strength. She coaxed him into revealing this, and while he was asleep, Delilah cut off his locks. The Philistines then captured and blinded him, and put him to work tied to a millstone to grind corn. However, Samson's hair grew again and, with God's help, he regained his former strength. Then, when led to the pillars of the temple of Dagon, he used his strength to push down the pillars, causing the temple to come crashing down on the heads of his Philistine enemies.

David—Another great Biblical hero is David, and his battle with the Philistine giant, Goliath. David was a mere slip of a boy, whereas the gigantic Goliath was the champion of the Philistines. They confronted each other, Goliath clad in armour and with weapons and shield, and David armed only with a slingshot. However, David's aim was true, and with a single stone he struck Goliath in the center of his forehead, and the giant came crashing to the ground, whereupon David immediately cut off his head and held it up high for all to see.

Robin Hood—Among medieval English legends, probably the most well-known is Robin Hood, who with his Merry Men, took up cudgels (or more appropriately, bows and arrows) on behalf of the poor peasants against the unscrupulous Sheriff of Nottingham. Our hero robbed from the rich to give to the poor. His band of outlaws included Will Scarlett, Little John, and Friar Tuck. Most of the action took place in Sherwood Forest, near Nottingham. In popular culture, Robin Hood was a supporter of the absent king, Richard the Lionheart, who was taking part in the Crusades. England, at that time, was under the rule of Richard's brother, Prince John, who was an unpopular ruler. Many ballads were written about Robin Hood and his exploits, which go back to the early part of the 15th century. A host of films have been made about the legend of this very popular English hero, so that his name and those of his Merry Men are very familiar to one and all. Sir Walter Scott's *Ivanhoe*, is also woven around this story.

King Arthur—The legend of King Arthur and the knights of his Round Table is also another very popular one in English folklore. Names like Camelot, and characters like the wizard Merlin, and Sir Lancelot and his love for Guinevere, have been the theme of various Hollywood films, like *Camelot* and also *Excalibur*, about a magical sword that was set in a stone, and whom only the chosen one, in this case the young Arthur, was able to withdraw.

Aladdin and his Lamp—In Middle-Eastern literature, the fable of Aladdin and his Lamp is a very well-known and popular one. In this tale, Aladdin is an impoverished young ne'er-do-well in a Chinese town who is tempted by a sorcerer into retrieving a precious oil-lamp from a magic cave that is guarded by all sorts of booby-trapped devices. When he finds the lamp and accidentally rubs it, a genie (djinn), that has been trapped in the lamp, pops out and has to grant Aladdin his wishes, and the boy ultimately becomes rich and powerful. This has also been the theme for many films.

Sinbad the Sailor—Another Middle-Eastern tale is about the seven voyages of Sinbad the Sailor. Here, our hero in the course of his voyages, has fantastic experiences in magical places, and encounters all sorts of monsters and supernatural phenomena. His adventures have been made into many films, animated cartoons, and TV series.

Superman—Modern day super-heroes include comic book characters like Superman. This super-being was sent to Earth as a child by his parents, as his home planet, Krypton, was under threat of destruction. A Kansas farmer and his wife discovered his space capsule, and raised him as Clark Kent. As an adult, he worked as a journalist for a Metropolis newspaper. He was endowed with the superhuman abilities of his species, like x-ray vision, super-hearing, the ability to fly at super-speed, the possession of super-strength, and invulnerability to attack by any kind of weapons. All these abilities he turns to good, in the fight against crime.

Batman—Is another crime-busting comic book super-hero. Unlike Superman, he was not super-human, but made use of his intellectual and martial art skills, science, and technology to invent and create fabulous vehicles like the Batmobile. He used his wealth and physical prowess on his continuous war on crime. Some of his arch-enemies were the Joker, the Penguin, the Riddler, and Catwoman. Batman went under the guise of Bruce Wayne, and was sometimes partnered by his young devotee, Robin, at least in earlier times. Probably owing to today's political correctness, it was not considered appropriate that such a relationship should exist between an older and younger man, so consequentially, Robin took very much a back-seat and has not been included in the more recent blockbuster movies featuring Batman.

Spiderman—Another popular comic-book character is Spiderman. A bite from a radioactive spider caused all sorts of physical changes in the body of young Peter Parker, giving him super-powers, such as the ability to cling to walls, superhuman strength, and a sixth or 'spider-sense' that alerted him to danger. He also had super-human speed and agility, balance, and equilibrium. He could also cast webs by shooting them out of his wrists, giving him the ability to swing and dangle in space. The young Peter dressed up in special Spiderman garb, which he sewed together to hide his true identity. Again, several blockbuster films have been made in recent years on the exploits of Spiderman.

Doctor Who—A very popular, and one of the longest running, British television series was Doctor Who. This intrepid and slightly eccentric Time Lord could travel through time in a machine called the Tardis, which was disguised as a blue police box, but once inside morphed into a space-time machine. The

Doctor met various challenges during the course of his time travels, including the dreaded Daleks, half-human, half-machine mutants, who seemed to have no other purpose other than to 'Exterminate! Exterminate! Exterminate!' Various actors throughout the series, which the BBC began in 1963, have played the part of the Doctor, and this fits into the scheme of things, as a process of regeneration is applicable to all Time Lords, who can change their personality or take on a new body, should their incarnation be damaged or injured in any way.

Among other mythical and fantastic creatures, in folklore and legend, are dragons, unicorns, and griffins. More humanoid creatures are such things as mermaids, fairies, gnomes, leprechauns, and hobgoblins.

Dragons—Have always featured prominently in medieval folklore. Think of St. George and the Dragon. Most cultures of the world give great significance to dragons, especially the Chinese and Japanese. They feature frequently in illustrations and paintings, and play a role in festivals like the Chinese New Year. They are also depicted frequently in Western art and in emblems, ensigns, and heraldry. Being serpent-like creatures, and breathing out fire and smoke, they appear both fearsome and awesome. They also feature regularly in computer games, films, and TV shows.

Fairies—Play an important role in European folklore and are featured in many children's books and stories. These creatures, that can include goblins, gnomes, elves, and sprites, are often referred to as 'the little people' by the Irish. These creatures are depicted as tiny or at least small, and humanoid in appearance, some having wings, and possessing magical qualities. They have been featured in famous plays, like William Shakespeare's *A Midsummer's Night Dream*, and the famous Tinker Bell, in J.M. Barrie's, *Peter Pan*. Quite a stir took place in the early part of the 20th century when two little girls claimed they had photographed fairies in their garden. Their claims were of great interest at the time, and were investigated by none other than the famous Sir Arthur Conan Doyle, creator of Sherlock Holmes. Of course, it all turned out to be a hoax.

Santa Claus—Is a fictional character that plays a significant role in folklore, particularly at Christmastime. He is also known as Saint Nicholas, Father Christmas, and Kris Kringle. Christmas would not be complete without the familiar, jovial, portly white-bearded character dressed in red, who appears on most Christmas cards and decorations. He is often depicted in his sleigh, drawn by his reindeer, delivering sacks of presents to all good little boys and girls. He is modelled on Saint Nicholas of Myra, a 4th century Greek bishop, famous for his generosity in distributing gifts to the poor.

There are also devilish and malevolent creations of the darker side of our imaginations, and these take the form of vampires, werewolves, ghouls, ghosts, and zombies. These have been dreamt up to stimulate our imagination and instil a sense of fear that is exciting and terrifying at the same time. Our psyche seems to demand a certain amount of terror to get the Adrenalin going—like eating a hot chilli.

Vampires—Horror movies featuring vampires are difficult to avoid now-a-days. **Count Dracula**, dreamt up by Bram Stoker in 1897, was modelled on a real and infamous character, Vlad the Impaler, a Transylvanian-born aristocrat who impaled his victims on wooden stakes. However, Bram Stoker's vampire is a blood-sucking creature with fangs, who bites his victims on the neck, and gorges himself with blood. Vampires can take the form of a bat, and the idea was probably conjured up on vampire bats that inhabit the forests from Mexico to Argentina and which mainly attack cattle. However, in Bram Stoker's version, the victims, once bitten by the vampire, become a vampire themselves, and are part of the living dead, who spend the daylight hours in coffins as they are averse to sunlight, which can destroy them.

Werewolves—Are very much part of European mythology, and the subject of many horror films. Traditionally, they are thought to be a human turned into a wolf-like creature due to a curse. They can revert to their human form, but at the onset of the full moon, turn into wolf-like monsters, attacking their victims, who in turn become werewolves.

Zombies—Another popular subject of horror films is Zombies. These seem to be based on myths originating in Africa and the Caribbean, through voodoo spells placed on them by medicine men. They are basically animated corpses raised by the dead through witchcraft, and in horror movies like *Night of the Living Dead*, attack and eat their victims.

Ghosts, Phantoms, and Spectres—Are also traditionally believed to be the spirits of the dead. This goes back to antiquity, and the spirits of the dead are often worshipped in some primitive cultures. In popular traditions, these spirits are thought to be earth-bound. In other words, if a person dies and his spirit is not at peace, he or she wanders around as a lost soul, often haunting living humans with their ghostly apparitions. Charles Dickens, in his *A Christmas Carol,* exploited this theme to change his character, Scrooge, from a mean old skinflint, into a generous and charitable person. Atheists, who according to their convictions do not believe in an after-life, would—I feel—be reluctant to spend a night in a cemetery on their own!

Our human experience would be dull indeed without the invention of these mythological characters, to stir up our imaginations and help liven up our earthly existence.

Where We Live

We are all inhabitants of planet Earth, which together with its neighbouring planets, circles around the Sun. This is known as the Solar System.

This System forms a very tiny part of a vast island of stars called the Milky Way galaxy, which is one of many billions of other galaxies that exist in the visible Universe. The Universe itself is thought to have been formed 14 billion years ago in an event called the Big Bang, when a minuscule point of energy, termed a singularity, 'exploded' and created all matter, time, and space in an instant. This scientific theory conflicts with Christian, Jewish, and Islamic religious belief, which considers that an all-divining god created the Universe in six days, and that the Earth was at the centre of it all.

This religious belief held sway until the 16th century, when early philosophers like Copernicus, and astronomers like Galileo, challenged this conception, and worked out that the Sun was at the centre of the Solar System and the known planets whirled around it. For their ideas, they faced persecution by the established Church. Not much later, such scientific giants as Sir Isaac Newton came on the scene and confirmed these theories. But the Universe itself was still something incomprehensible, until in the 20th century scientific geniuses like Albert Einstein and Edwin Hubble made some sense of it all.

This comparatively small planet is our homeland and gives us everything we need to survive—the air that we breathe, the water that we drink, and the food that we eat. Our Sun gives us light, heat, and energy, without which we would not be able to exist.

Earth is the only planet in the vast Universe where we know for certain that life exists, and it does so in abundance—from microscopic bacteria that live on every speck of dust or drop of water, to plants, insects, fish, reptiles, animals, and us humans. As far as we know, none of our neighbouring planets have any life whatsoever—not even a bacterium.

Not only does our planet supply our food and other means of sustenance, but also the Earth itself provides a wealth of minerals and chemicals, which we have been able to manipulate to forge our metals and make into products. We have 92 elements found on Earth, out of which we can make anything from a sewing needle to an atomic bomb!

The Solar System contains eight planets. The first four being the inner planets, and small rocky ones. These are Mercury, Venus, Earth, and Mars. The remaining four are the outer planets: Jupiter, Saturn, Uranus, and Neptune. They are not small and rocky but are giant balls of gas, which do not have a solid surface.

Earth is the only planet in the Solar System to have land-masses and oceans, where both terrestrial and aquatic life can exist.

It is not surprising that the ancients thought the world was the centre of the Universe, as it is all-important to us. Besides the Sun, we may not need the rest of the Universe in order to survive. Indeed, if it had been hidden to us throughout our history—say our skies had been continuously cloudy with not even a star peeking through, we would not have been aware of the vast Universe that surrounds us. In such a scenario, philosophical and scientific thought might never have gotten underway, because it was wondering about the stars and planets and what they were that got us all thinking. So we should all be grateful for clear and starry skies!

As it stands, we are just a mere pale blue dot when viewed from the fringes of the Solar System, lost among the hundreds of millions of stars of the Milky Way, and so insignificant that if it suddenly disappeared, it would not be noticed at all.

Our Earth is sometimes referred to as the 'Goldilocks planet' because its orbit around the Sun is at just the right distance for liquid water to exist. Also, it spins on its axis once every 24 hours at an angle of 23½ degrees, which gives us not only night and day but also our seasons. This is just about the right speed, because if it was to spin more slowly, it could roast on one side and freeze on the other, like the planet Mercury does. Its tilt, as it journeys around the Sun once in every 365 days, is just sufficient to make our seasons of spring, summer, autumn, and winter sufficiently long, at intervals of three months each. This is enough to allow plants to grow and be harvested, to ensure good crops. Our weather system ensures sufficient rainfall for a plentiful supply of fresh water, distilled in the clouds from the seas, lakes, and rivers. Were it not for this, our planet would be a barren desert like Mars.

Of course, sometimes disaster strikes, and there are storms, floods, droughts, earthquakes, and landslides and the like, and in olden days the gods were thought to be in control of all these events. These natural disasters are a cause of great concern, and result in enormous damage and loss of life. We do not yet have the technology to control our weather or accurately predict earthquakes. Therefore, these events often catch us off-guard, though our weather satellites are a great help in predicting where typhoons and hurricanes can hit.

We humans cannot survive in the open environment as so many of our animal friends can. So we sheltered in caves then began to build houses, which became villages, towns, and cities. Also, we coped with the darkness of night by building fires, then burning candles, and eventually with the discovery of electricity, we literally lit up the globe and made night-time friendlier for us. Satellite images of the world at night reveal how lit up certain parts of the globe appear.

We have explored virtually the whole of our world. We have navigated the oceans; we have explored the continents; we have climbed the highest mountains; we have descended into the depths of the deepest oceans; we have reached the limits of our atmosphere. Now, we have gone beyond the Earth and landed men on the Moon. With our spacecraft, we have journeyed to the limits of the Solar System itself, and are currently exploring planets like Mars with robotic vehicles.

Now we are turning towards the stars in the search for other habitable planets, for should our world or our species ever be threatened by extinction, we would have somewhere else to go. But the technical aspects of such a journey are awesome, and we may never be able to achieve this.

In the meantime, we must try to preserve this little planet and not pollute our atmosphere and oceans with poisons and chemicals. It is the only home we have, and if we do not take care of this fragile and precious bubble of life, we shall do so at our peril.

Explorers, Navigators, and Colonisers

During the course of his tenure on Earth, mankind has never stayed in one place, but has continuously wandered around the planet. From the time our ancient ancestors migrated out of Africa, humans have sought new habitats and pastures, spreading across the face of the Earth like an ink stain on blotting paper.

Some animals, particularly domesticated dogs and cats, have been taken with us on our travels, and vermin—like rats—have always followed us around, because wherever we settled there was always some food source to be found. But some animals stuck to particular regions of the planet where their habitat was favourable. For example, you will not find chimpanzees out of the African continent, and you will not find tigers outside Asia. On the other hand, Man went everywhere—the same species (homo-sapiens), but perhaps altered in colour and appearance, depending on where they settled. For example, a black skin is better able to cope with the fierce sunlight in hot countries than a white skin, which is more suitable for cooler climes. Our early competitor, Neanderthal man, migrated to the Near East, Central Asia, and into Europe, where he died out 20 to 30 thousand years ago. This was probably due to his inability to compete with the superior species, homo-sapiens, although there is some DNA evidence to show that Neanderthals and homo-sapiens might have mated and produced mixed offspring. Fossilised remains were discovered in the Neander Valley in Germany, and were thus named 'Neanderthal man' by geologist William King in 1864.

Not long after the first civilizations were established, maps showing surrounding territories began to be drawn—some of the oldest surviving ones being Babylonian maps from the 9th century B.C. The use of maps became a helpful aid in finding one's way around, particularly by ancient seafarers like the Egyptians, Phoenicians, and Greeks for trade and other purposes.

Ancient mariners usually hugged the coast to travel from place to place. They still had the conviction that the world was flat, and that if they ventured too far out they would fall off. Following the coastline was also a useful navigational aid. The wind and a battery of oars usually powered the vessels they used for their travels. They also used the stars to guide them, and managed to find their way around the Mediterranean. Written records using stars for navigation go as far back as Homer's Odyssey. Nautical charts and sailing directions were in use as early as the 6th century B.C. Evidence of other nautical aids they used was the discovery in 1900 of the Antikythera mechanism from the wreck of an ancient Greek ship, a complicated brass instrument of cogs and wheels, which is thought to have been built around the 1st century B.C.

Once seafarers were reassured that the world was spherical and not flat, Christopher Columbus, an Italian explorer and navigator, with the support of Spanish monarchs Ferdinand II and Isabella, sailed out West across the Atlantic with three ships in search of a shorter route to the East Indies in pursuance of the lucrative spice trade. Of course, he did not know at the time that the vast continents of the Americas lay between him and his objective, so he stumbled across this vast land-mass in 1492, not realising what it was, and assuming he had reached his destination, he called the inhabitants 'Indians', by which name they are still referred to until this day. The discovery of America was one of the most important geographical finds ever and eventually led to its colonisation.

Seafaring really took off with the explorations undertaken by the Portuguese in the 15th century, when they took the lead in long distance oceanic navigation. Seafarers, like Vasco da Gama, landed on the coast of India (Goa) in 1498. This was to establish a route for the spice trade. Spices like pepper, cinnamon, cloves, etc., were rare and expensive commodities in the West, and much sought after to improve the flavour of food. His travels took him as far as the island of Macau in South-East Asia, which remained a Portuguese colony as recently as 1999.

Ferdinand Magellan, a Portuguese explorer, was also in search of a route to the Spice Islands in Indonesia. Between the years 1519—1522, he sailed southwards over the Atlantic, and reached the tip of South America where he sailed through a passage, the Strait of Magellan, which was named after him. He was the first explorer to sail from the Atlantic Ocean to the Pacific, and his voyage, completed by Juan Sebastian Elcano, (because sadly Magellan was killed in the Philippines), heralded the first circumnavigation of the Earth.

Captain James Cook, a British explorer, navigator, and cartographer, made three voyages to the Pacific Ocean between 1768 and 1779. His first voyage, in The Endeavour, was to the island of Tahiti to observe the transit of the planet Venus across the face of the Sun. In this voyage and subsequent voyages across the Pacific, he made detailed maps of largely-uncharted areas of the globe, including New Zealand and Australia. He went in search of the Southern Continent, which was thought to exist somewhere in that region, and which supposedly covered much of the Southern Hemisphere, including Australia, Antarctica, and many of the Polynesian Islands. He travelled widely over the Pacific Ocean, from the boundaries of Antarctica to the entrance of the Saint Lawrence River in Canada, mapping the land areas as he progressed on his voyages. Tragically, he was killed in a conflict with the Hawaiian islanders in 1779.

What made these extensive voyages possible were the great improvements in navigational techniques, with the help of instruments like the compass, the sextant, and—later—extremely accurate clocks, such as the chronometer. The globe was divided into grids, with horizontal lines called lines of latitude, and vertical lines from the poles, called longitude. The horizontal belt across the middle of the globe was called the Equator, and divided the Northern and Southern hemispheres. These gridlines were marked in degrees of longitude and latitude, and time measurement was taken from the Greenwich Meridian line that ran through the Royal Observatory in Greenwich, London. The International Date Line ran down on the opposite side of the globe, through the Pacific Ocean.

Not only were the oceans explored, but also the continents, with explorers like Marco Polo, a merchant from Venice, who travelled from Italy across Asia to China; and Livingstone and Burton who explored the African continent in search of the source of the River Nile.

Spanish exploration and colonisation began in South America in the 1500s by Spanish conquistadors, like Cortez and Pizarro. And ancient cultures, such as the Aztecs, Incas, and Mayans living there, were completely overwhelmed and decimated in the conquistadors' search for gold, and later by missionaries with their desire to convert the 'heathen' natives to Catholicism.

Wherever they went, the Europeans took their diseases with them, and when settlers such as the Pilgrim Fathers from Plymouth, England, colonised New England on the north-east coast of America in 1620, they discovered that the Patuxent people, who had hitherto occupied the region, had either run away or been wiped out by a series of plagues. Thus, the Native American people, who had populated the continent, were eventually decimated, falling victim to diseases like smallpox and syphilis. With the spread of Western civilization, and inevitable wars and conflicts, some of the Native

Americans were driven further westward, until the 'West was won', and Indian tribes like the Apaches, Crowe, Sioux, and Comanche were driven out of their lands to live in 'Reservations' where some still exist today, although there are many who live among the general population of the United States.

When Australia was colonised by the British, starting at Botany Bay in 1778 as a penal colony, the native Aboriginals were also displaced and now mainly live in small communities in remote regions of the continent. Their ancient culture did not have what we call a 'work ethic', so they usually live in impoverished circumstances, though the Australian government have made efforts to assist and assimilate them into the social structure of modern-day Australia. In earlier times, half-caste offspring of these Aboriginals were required to live on Reserves or Missions, work for their provisions, given minimal education, and had to seek permission to marry, visit relatives, or even to use electrical appliances!

The Australian Aboriginal was more fortunate than their neighbouring Tasmanian cousins, as these indigenous occupants of Tasmania were completely wiped out by wars with European settlers and the diseases they brought with them, and the last full-blooded Tasmanian survivor was a woman named Truganini, who finally died in 1876, thus bringing an end to their race.

In India, colonisation took a more stealthy form by the British, establishing a trading company called the East India

Company, in (mainly) Bombay, Madras, and Calcutta. Since India was a very civilized culture under the Moghuls, the British formed allegiances with Indian maharajas, and assisted the more friendly ones in their wars with their neighbours. As in North America, the British carried their conflicts with the French to the Indian sub-continent, and never allowed them to establish any significant foothold there, except perhaps, Pondicherry—a small territory on the Eastern coast, and Chandanagore—a small area outside Calcutta. Eventually, after the Indian Mutiny in 1857, when the native Indian sepoys rebelled against their British masters, leading to a blood-bath of massacres, the British took control of most of the country, and put it under the British Crown. Queen Victoria became the first Empress of India, and it became the 'jewel in the crown' of the British Empire for almost a hundred years, until India was given full independence in 1947.

In Africa, various European countries gained a foothold— the British; the Belgians; the Germans; the French; the Portuguese; the Spanish; the Italians. Eventually, these foreign powers relinquished control, beginning in the 1950s, but in their wake they left their former colonies (that formed Africa) in a total shambles, and conflicts still exist between the various races that live on that continent, with frequent power-struggles and ethnic troubles.

We can conclude that the explorations by these Western pioneers shaped our planet into the civilization that exists in the world today.

Builders and Constructors

We humans have always been builders and constructors. Give an infant a set of blocks, and he or she will immediately begin to stack them to form some sort of structure. Building projects have always been a challenge for us humans, as we are constantly fighting the effects of gravity, which makes things want to topple over as soon as they get tall enough. This has been the struggle that our ancestors have always had to try to overcome with special building techniques. However, overcome them we have, and our great buildings, bridges, and other structures stand tall as evidence of our success.

Buildings

When they left their caves, early humans made habitats where they could live and be protected from the elements, as unlike our animal friends who could survive quite easily out in the open, Man needed shelter in order to survive. It protected him from the cold, sheltered him from the sun, rain, and wind, and gave him a safe habitat from likely predators.

The earliest houses were simple affairs. All had walls and a roof, a door for access, and perhaps a window or two to let in some light. They usually took the form of huts, and were built from whatever building material they had to hand at the time—stones, logs or mud, with a roof of sorts made from thatch, moss, or some form of tiles. In some societies, animal hides and other materials were used to make tents. The Eskimos even used ice to make their igloos.

Once again, religion played a significant role in the construction of enormous building projects, like the ancient Egyptian pyramids, and temples for the worship of gods and other deities. Some of the most ancient structures, like the temple at Göbekli Tepe, were made mainly for some religious reasons. These ancient structures were made mostly of carved stone blocks precisely placed and assembled by enormous human effort. Not only were the pyramids constructed this way, but also the ancient terraced walls at Saksaywaman in Peru, South America, by the ancient Inca people.

As all schoolchildren will have learned, the Seven Wonders of the Ancient World included such gigantic structures as the Great Pyramid of Giza, the Hanging Gardens of Babylon, the Statue of Zeus at Olympia, the Colossus of Rhodes, and the Lighthouse of Alexandria. Of these great structures, only the Great Pyramid survives. All these structures took great planning and building skills, and most of them had some religious significance. Even the beautiful Taj Mahal in India was built as a mausoleum for the wife of the Moghul Ruler, Shah Jehan. Other examples of huge structures, like temples, mosques, and cathedrals, can be found all over the world, like the largest Hindu temple of Angkor in Cambodia, the Parthenon in Athens, Hagia Sophia in Istanbul, and St. Peter's Basilica in the Vatican. Of course, some great ancient structures, like the Coliseum in Rome, were built not for religious purposes, but as an amphitheatre for entertainment purposes, like throwing Christians to the lions!

The invention and use of concrete helped greatly in the construction of great buildings, with arches, vaults, and domes. This material quickly hardened into a rigid mass and joined stones together, even underwater, which was very useful for the construction of bridges by the ancient Romans. It is still used in the form of reinforced concrete for some of the largest buildings in the world today.

Now-a-days, commerce has taken pride of place over religion, and some of the largest buildings in the world are mainly for offices and hotels. The Empire State building in New York held the record of the highest skyscraper in the world for forty years, until the Twin Towers of the World Trade Centre superseded it in 1970. These were tragically destroyed by the terrible events of 11th September 2001, when Al Qaeda terrorists crashed two passenger airliners into them.

Today, New York has surrendered its title of having the tallest skyscraper to Dubai where the 'Burj Khalifa' towers to a height of 2,717 feet. Other cities, like Kaula Lumpur in Malaysia, also have one of the tallest buildings—the Petronas Tower at 1,483 feet. But Chicago still has the formerly named Sears Tower, at 1,450 feet—the highest building in the United States.

Today, vast cities, towns, and villages have been constructed all over the world, built by the hand of Man, albeit with the help of heavy machinery, unlike the ancients who had only their muscle power to undertake their massive building projects.

Roads and Railways

When our ancient ancestors came out of Africa and migrated over the globe, they must have encountered many problems in their wanderings. There were no roads or trails to follow, and in their journey across the continents, they must have faced many problems and obstacles, like rivers, mountains, and deserts, which all had to be avoided and skirted around, as they had no bridges or boats. However, after primitive settlements were established, pathways and trails were made and followed to connect them to the nearest neighbouring village, and later on these became permanent trails or roads. The history of road building goes back aeons— the oldest known paved road being laid by the ancient Egyptians 4,500 years ago. Stone paved streets, a necessity to avoid trudging in the mud, have been found in the Middle East, dating back to about the same time. Wooden planks and logs were also used as paving, and the timber track-way in England is one of the oldest engineered roads discovered in Northern Europe, going back 5 millennia. India used brick paving as early as 3,000 B.C.

The Romans took the lead in road building, mainly to move their armies and transport goods, and after the Roman invasion of Britain, they constructed a network of paved roads to connect the important cities and towns they occupied. The saying, 'all roads lead to Rome,' was particularly relevant in the case of Britain.

Over the millennia, a network of roads spread all over the civilized world. This not only helped travellers get to their destinations by carriage and coach, and later by motor vehicles, but was also the lifeblood for the transportation of goods and merchandise.

With the invention of the steam engine, a network of railway tracks also began to be built all over the world, and the construction of these railway lines, such as the First Transcontinental Railway to traverse North America, was one of the greatest engineering feats of the 19th century, as it entailed the laying of hundreds of miles of rail track over difficult terrain and through tunnels blasted out of mountainsides.

Bridges

Crossing rivers and streams was always a problem for the ancients. Only with the construction of bridges were people able to ford these obstacles, mainly for travel purposes and for the military that needed to move troops over rivers and streams in large numbers. Initially, man made use of bridges made by nature, such as a log that had accidentally fallen across a stream, or stepping-stones in a small river. The first bridges made by humans would have been lengths of cut wooden logs or planks, and eventually stones.

The greatest bridge-builders were the ancient Romans, who designed and built arch bridges and aqueducts which could stand up to conditions that would damage or destroy earlier designs. Other cultures used various types of bridges suitable for their purpose, making use of materials readily available, like rope-suspension bridges to cross swiftly-flowing mountain torrents. The use of such bridges goes back to antiquity, and the ancient Inca civilization made these rope suspension bridges prior to European colonisation in the 16th century. In the 18th century, there were many innovations and designs for timber bridges, but it was really with the discovery of cast iron that a major breakthrough in bridge-building technology took place, such as the construction of the Iron Bridge in England in 1779.

With the dawning of the Industrial Revolution in the 19th century, wrought iron became commonly used for the erection of larger bridges, but this did not have the tensile strength to support large loads. It was only with the advent of steel, with its high tensile strength, that much larger bridges could be built.

Various types of bridges were designed and built, from simple beam bridges (such as a deck supported by pillars), to arch bridges (the deck supported by an arch underneath), and then to cantilever bridges (constructed with girders and beams with both ends of the deck fixed to the embankment), and suspension bridges (the deck being suspended by cables that are fixed to tall towers at both ends). The Golden Gate Bridge in San Francisco is a good example of a suspension bridge, and is probably one of the most well known in the world today.

Tunnels

Tunnelling probably first began with ancient civilizations like the Romans building sewers and drainage systems for their towns and cities to improve sanitation. But later, when humans confronted obstacles that could not be bridged or forded, they used this technology to tunnel. We have bored through mountains and underwater to create a passage through or underneath these obstacles. Tunnels like the Lincoln Tunnel beneath the Hudson River, to connect Manhattan and New Jersey in the USA, is just one example of our tunnelling skills. We have even burrowed below cities to create subways like the London Underground and New York Subway. Massive projects, like the Channel Tunnel have been completed using huge boring machines to create a subterranean passage beneath the English Channel, connecting the United Kingdom to Europe. This high-speed rail link opened in 1994.

Canals

Canals, like the Suez and Panama canals were also massive engineering undertakings, and were necessary to facilitate shipping. The Suez canal (opened in 1869) was cut between the Mediterranean and Red Sea, and this shortened the sea voyage between Europe and Asia considerably, as hitherto, ships had to travel all the way around the Cape of Good Hope. The Panama canal (opened in 1914) cut through the narrow land strip between North and South America. This route connected the Atlantic and Pacific oceans, and avoided the long and treacherous sea voyage around Cape Horn—a nightmare for intrepid sailors and their vulnerable sailing ships that attempted this dangerous passage.

Ship Building

The seas and oceans were another great challenge for the ancients to overcome. Whereas early humans had to traverse the continents on foot, (the continent of North America was thought to have been connected to the landmass of Asia at that time by a strip of land where the Bearing Strait is located), their ancient descendants needed a means of travelling across the seas and oceans. Hence, they built boats and ships. The earliest archaeological evidence of humans crossing the seas was the arrival of natives from the Asian mainland to Borneo at least 30,000 years ago in their canoes, when, during an ice age period, sea levels were lower and distances shorter between islands. These ancient mariners certainly seemed to know their way about, and eventually spread south as far as Australia and New Zealand.

Ancient Egyptians constructed their ships from cedar wood, with a single mast and a square sail on a yard. These ships could also be propelled through the water by oars. The Phoenicians and Greeks had similar sorts of ships and with these were able to traverse the Mediterranean. The Romans, on the other hand, were not much of a sea-faring nation, and relied mainly on their nautically inclined subjects, the Greeks and Egyptians, to build and man their ships. They seemed to prefer to have their legions march across the land to conquer and occupy.

Sea-faring people, like the Vikings, used their vessels to great effect in crossing the seas to England, where they partly conquered the island and ruled for a time. There is evidence to show that the ancient Vikings also reached North America in their vessels long before the Portuguese, as also to the Mediterranean and Africa, and to the east to Russia, and perhaps even further! The Portuguese, Spanish, and British, were also great seafarers, and the ships they built were capable of traversing the open oceans. These were multi-sailed vessels with masts of the strongest timber, and mainly took the form of warships equipped with cannon. The Spanish galleons were enormous ships for that time, and could be equipped with over 300 cannons. With these ships, the great seafaring nations could traverse the world and carry out their explorations and, of course, wars.

Outside Medieval Europe, cultures like the Chinese and Arabs also made great advances in shipbuilding, and some of their commercial vessels, mainly those of the Chinese, reached a size and sophistication exceeding that of contemporary Europe. The mainstay of China's merchant fleet was the junk. The Arabs, too, were great seafarers and their dhows were quite capable of travelling the oceans.

With the advent of steam, and ships being constructed from metal rather than wood, shipbuilding really took off, and the canvas sail could finally be dispensed with. The shipyards of

England, Europe, America, and more recently, Japan, were busily occupied building large ocean-going vessels for both commerce and war. Steam ships were still going strong as recently as the middle part of the 20th century, then diesel engines began to take over, which dispensed with the need for coal-fired furnaces to heat the steam boilers—a very labour-intensive business.

Today, we build gigantic ships, both for commerce and war. The transport of passengers in the past relied mostly on ships to travel between the continents, and huge ocean liners were built. The most memorable of which was the ill-fated Titanic, which collided with an iceberg and sank in the Atlantic on its maiden voyage from Southampton to New York in 1912, resulting in the tragic loss of 1,500 souls, mostly male passengers and crew. Now-a-days, passenger travel is mostly by air, but huge cruise ships are still being constructed for holiday cruises. Enormous ships like the gigantic oil-tankers are still the main means of transporting oil between the oil-producing countries and the rest of the world, and also huge container ships are used for carrying goods. Since the 1950s, some ships are nuclear-powered, like the SS Savanah built as a passenger-carrying cargo ship. Some warships and ice-breakers have also been put into service by countries like the USA and former USSR. This form of power dispenses with the need for regular re-fuelling, and is used particularly for submarines to extend their range and capabilities.

These are just some of the accomplishments we humans have managed to make that have changed our planet beyond all recognition. From satellite images taken from space, we can see our great cities, ports, and harbours. Even the Great Wall of China, one of the biggest building projects ever undertaken, can be seen from space. Our ingenuity and building skills have made all this possible, and we have shrunk the world and made it a habitable place for us to live in comfort, with the ease of access to reach even the most remote places.

Artists, Musicians, and Writers

Painting and Sculpture

Humans have always displayed a need to express themselves and pictorially represent the world around them. From earliest times, paintings, such as those on cave walls, depicted hunting scenes, with pictures of humans, and animals like reindeer, mammoths, horses, and bison. These are thought to serve as part of a 'magic' ritual to ensure a successful hunt. All this was done in the darkness of caves using smoky lamps of animal fat, and applying the simplest of earth pigments, like ochres.

They also produced carved ornaments, such as figurines and beads, and engravings on stones and pottery. Religious belief had not yet taken a prominent role, so they confined their art to familiar things in their experience. However, a statuette of carved limestone called 'the Venus of Willendorf', dating from around 21,000 B.C., was found at a Palaeolithic site in Lower Austria in 1908. It shows an exaggerated bulbous female figure, and is thought to be a fertility symbol with some sort of magical significance.

Some of the finest examples of paintings that have survived through the ages are those of the ancient Egyptians. Owing to the highly religious nature of this early civilization, their work depicted their gods and goddesses, as also Pharaohs, who were considered divine. Their drawings were simple and two-dimensional with flat areas of vivid colour. These were done on limestone walls of tombs covered with a fine layer of plaster, onto which they painted their various scenes, using pigments of different colours. These paintings have given us an insight into the culture of this ancient civilization.

In classical Greece, sculptures seemed to predominate, as also paintings on pottery. Greek art stayed mainly confined to their various gods and goddesses and mythical heroes, as depicted in statues and paintings on pottery. Most of the statues and paintings showed the human body in complete nudity, and some were of an erotic nature. Greek art had a significant influence on the Romans, who also followed the same pattern and style, and Roman emperors became the subject of many of these Roman works of art.

In the Byzantine period, Christ took centre stage in iconic mosaics done at that time. The Madonna and Child was also another popular subject for artists, like Raphael, and there are many depictions of Mary and baby Jesus going back to Byzantine times. Strangely, in almost all paintings of the infant Jesus, he is shown uncircumcised, whereas we learn from the Gospel of Luke that he was circumcised on the eighth day, according to Jewish tradition. Christ himself is often depicted as European-looking, sometimes with fair hair and blue eyes; whereas it is almost certain that he was of a darker skin colour and more Middle-Eastern in appearance. The same goes for his mother, Mary.

As always, the Church played a dominant part in the world of art in the time of the High Renaissance, and in 1508, Pope Julias II commissioned the famous painter and sculptor,

Michelangelo Buonarroti, to paint the ceiling of the Sistine Chapel in the Vatican. The entire ceiling was painted with religious frescoes from the Creation of Adam to the Last Judgment. This was probably the largest undertaking by any artist, and it took Michelangelo four years to complete the project, which stands out as one of the largest commissions by the Church to any individual artist. Of course, the Church was exceedingly rich, more so than any wealthy aristocrat, and so art was dedicated mostly to religious themes during the High Renaissance. It was also a sign of the Church's wealth and power. Not only did the Church commission the painting of the Sistine Chapel Ceiling to this great artist, but also the statues of Moses and David—two of the most well-known statues of any Biblical figures to this day.

During the High Renaissance, two other great painters emerged. These were Raphael, renowned for his beautiful paintings of the Madonnas, and Leonardo Da Vinci who was most celebrated for his masterpiece of the Last Supper. Sadly, this great work, showing Jesus and his disciples celebrating the Passover, was done using a technique of tempera over a ground of gesso, instead of the more reliable method of fresco on fresh plaster, such as Michelangelo employed for the Sistine Chapel Ceiling. As such, it has been deteriorating rapidly through the ages, with mould and flaking. However, Leonardo's most famous painting of all time, done with oil paint on white Lombardy poplar, is the Mona Lisa—'the lady with the mystic smile'—and, thankfully for a change, not on a religious theme!

In Europe in the 17th and 18th centuries, many famous artists came to prominence, such as the Dutch artists Johannes Vermeer and Rembrandt van Rijn. They painted mostly with oil paints on canvas, and chose more ordinary subjects like Vermeer's *The Milkmaid* and *the Girl with the Pearl Earring*, and Rembrandt's *Night Watch* and *Man in a Golden Helmet*. Other artists rose to fame like Jean Antoine Watteau (France), Antonio Canaletto (Italy), Sir Joshua Reynolds, Thomas Gainsborough, and William Hogarth (England). These artists also diverged from religious themes, and painted instead landscapes, and portraits of prominent people of their day. The scenes of Venice and its canals by Canaletto, and the *Blue Boy* by Gainsborough are a few of the more well-known paintings by these famous artists. Even animals began to be the subject for artists like George Stubbs, an English painter, who was famous for his paintings of horses.

In the latter part of the 19th century, a group of French artists in Paris began a movement called 'Impressionism'. It is thought that the movement was influenced by the paintings of Eugene Delacroix and J.M.W. Turner, who employed bolder painting techniques. The Impressionist painting method diverted from earlier paintings that had hitherto carefully blended and glazed colours to give the painting the quality of a well-mellowed violin. Here, brilliant colours were used with little effort made to disguise the brush strokes. The paintings were bold and spontaneous, with daubs of unblended paint. Among the well-known artists of this movement were: Pierre-Auguste Renior, Claude Monet, Édouard Manet, Paul Cézanne, and Edgar Degas. Followers of the movement were such famous artists as Georges Seurat, Henri de Toulouse-Lautrec, Paul Gaugin (famous for his paintings of Tahitian natives), and of course, the most famous of all, Dutch painter Vincent van Gogh.

However, this movement was way ahead of its time for the conservative society of that part of the century, when Queen Victoria still ruled from the throne of England, and the values of stern discipline and the stiff-upper-lip were very much in vogue. So consequently, these Impressionist painters had problems in exhibiting and selling their work, particularly in the case of Van Gogh, who only sold one painting in his lifetime, and had to live in impoverished circumstances with the help of his brother, Theo. He was a vigorous painter and would often finish a painting in a day. He squeezed paint fresh from the tubes, and daubed it directly on the canvas, sometimes using the handle of the brush. He was an eccentric person and suffered from periods of madness, and once cut off his left ear for the sake of a prostitute. His most well-known works are his paintings of sunflowers, which are worth hundreds of millions of pounds on the market today.

In the 20th century, with the development of photography, artists no longer felt the need to produce life-like images, which the camera could do more accurately, but began an avant-garde movement of representing the world around them more symbolically. Artists like the Spanish painter, Pablo Picasso, invented Cubism, a style of representing images of people and places in almost geometric facets that overlap and interlock with each other. Among his most famous paintings was *Guernica*, which depicted the inhumanity, brutality, and hopelessness of war—mainly the Spanish Civil War, which broke out in 1936. This large canvas was painted in oils, using only black and white, and is almost like a collage of images depicting the horrors of war. Other artistic movements followed, such as Futurism, Expressionism, and Surrealism. The most renowned Surrealist painter was Salvador Dali, whose best-known work was *The Persistence of Memory*, which shows surrealistic images of soft, melting pocket watches. One of the most famous works of contemporary modern art is *The Scream*, painted by Edvard Munch in 1893.

Today, no holds are barred to the modern-day artist. All techniques are employed, such as dribbling cans of paint on canvas, or splattering different colours on it and letting them merge naturally. Even a black square with a white dot at the centre is considered Modern Art, and most of these paintings are displayed in exhibitions and carry a price-tag of several hundreds of thousands of pounds. Some of these artists have a high status in the art world, like American 'pop-artist' Andy Warhol, famous for his almost 'comic-book' rendition of Marilyn Monroe, and his Campbell Soup tins.

Music

From earliest times, man always had a fondness for sounds that were pleasant to the ear, whether this took the form of rhythmic beats or melodious notes. Songbirds were always musical, and it was perhaps by imitating these birdsongs that early man developed a liking for musical sound. Initially, rhythm could be produced merely by clicking sounds from the tongue, the clapping of hands, and hitting stones together. The human voice, with its wide range of sound, was also a means of producing sound and song, by way of singing, humming, and chanting. The drum and flute were probably the simplest musical instruments to make, such as using a hollow log fitted with a membrane of animal skin stretched across each end to produce drumbeats, or a bamboo reed to make a simple type of flute. A stringed instrument could also be quite simply made, by twanging a length of dried and twisted animal gut on some sort of soundboard, or scraping it with a bow. These early musical instruments, mainly drums, are still used, particularly in primitive cultures—in Africa, among the native Indians of the Americas, and Pacific islanders.

All cultures had their particular form of music—India, China, and Japan. But to concentrate more on Western music, this really began in earnest with the Church, particularly in the form of chants going back to medieval times. Also, village communities used music and dance to celebrate their festivals. This developed into sophisticated forms, in palace courts and the halls of kings. In the time of Henry VIII of England, for instance, music and dance was a commonplace event, and Henry himself is thought to have composed the music and lyrics of the very well-known folk song, *Greensleeves*.

Western music really took off in the 18th and 19th centuries with great composers like Bach, Chopin, Debussy, Mozart, and Beethoven. Here, a wide range of musical instruments were employed to interpret the music into full orchestral renditions. Great operas and performances were put on to entertain the rich and famous, using both voice and musical accompaniment. Among the most-known of these were *The Marriage of Figaro*, *The Magic Flute*, and *Don Giovanni*, all by Mozart, and *The Barber of Seville* (Rossini), *La Traviata* (Verdi), and *La Bohème* (Puccini). These are but a few of the more popular ones.

In the 19th and 20th centuries, great composers like Johann Strauss wrote such famous waltzes as *The Blue Danube, Tales from the Vienna Woods*, and *The Emperor Waltz*. And, among his operettas, was the very popular *Die Fledermaus*. Later in the mid-20th century, came the great American composer George Gershwin, with his famous operetta *Porgy & Bess*, and his other well-known concerto *Rhapsody in Blue*. He also wrote *An American in Paris*, which was made into a Hollywood musical in 1951, starring Gene Kelly and Leslie Caron. It was a great tragedy and loss to the world of music when this brilliant composer died prematurely in 1937, aged only 38 years. However, his brother Ira, who wrote the lyrics for his musical compositions, continued in his career until the 1980s. The two brothers, George and Ira, wrote some of the most memorable

songs of the 20th century—songs like *I Got Rhythm,*
Embraceable You, The Man I Love, and *Someone to Watch Over*
Me. Although the lyrics for his famous song *Summertime* were
written by DuBose Heyward, the author of *Porgy.*

The developments of not only music, but also the varied
musical instruments that have been devised to create all the
range of musical tones, have brought such great pleasure to
our ears. These musical instruments produce their sound by
banging, blowing, twanging, and scraping—much like our
primitive ancestors used to do to produce musical sound.
These orchestral instruments are divided into classes—
percussion, brass, woodwinds, strings, and keyboard.
Percussion (banging) instruments take the form of timpani,
bass drum, triangles, and cymbals. Brass instruments (blowing)
are such things as trumpets, trombones, tubas, and horns
(French or English). Woodwinds (again blowing) are flutes,
oboes, clarinets, bassoons, and saxophones. Strings (twanging
or scraping) are harps, violins, cellos, double basses, and
guitars. Keyboards—which our ancient ancestors were not able
to produce, are harpsichords and pianos, as also pipe and
electronic organs.

Basically, music notations comprise of seven notes and
their respective sharps and flats, in a number of octaves. These
notations show the different sounds and pitches that can be
made. By combining these notes in certain sequences, millions
of songs can be played. The notation of music uses a five-line
staff, and the notes are placed along the staff. Duration is

shown with different note values and additional symbols, such as dots and ties. Using this system, any tune can be played, even if the player rendering the piece is unfamiliar with the song.

The world of music has brought great joy to our ears, and the Church especially has used music to praise the Lord. Such great compositions as Handel's *Messiah*, and the various hymns sung at church services, and carols sung at Christmas, have all enlivened our human experience.

Literature

As far as literature is concerned, we do not have to go back in history to Neolithic Man, because, of course, the written word did not exist as a means of communication or human expression. Although the ancient Egyptians had a pictorial text in the form of hieroglyphs, this was not adequate enough to write great works of literature.

Literature is defined as 'creative writing of recognised artistic value'. As such, I shall attempt to confine this section to writings worthy of purely artistic merit. I list only a few of the most prominent and recognised authors and their work, in chronological order.

Homer 8th century B.C.

Literature really took off with the legendary Greek poet, Homer, and his epic accounts of the Trojan War in *The Iliad* and *The Odyssey*, which were written at about the end of the 8th century B.C. Prior to that, possibly many ancient Greek scrolls would have been written, which could have been classed as literature, but these were all lost forever in the fire that consumed the library at Alexandria in the 1st century B.C.

Geoffrey Chaucer (1340 – 1400)

His greatest masterpiece was *The Canterbury Tales*, an account of pilgrims on their way to Canterbury, England, to pay homage at the shrine of Thomas á Becket, the Archbishop of Canterbury who was murdered at the cathedral in 1170 by followers of King Henry II of England, and became a saint and martyr. Chaucer was the greatest and most influential poet of the Middle Ages.

William Shakespeare (1564 – 1616)

Shakespeare was the greatest dramatist, poet, and playwright of Elizabethan England. His works are many and varied, and include such plays as *Hamlet, Macbeth, Romeo and Juliet, The Merchant of Venice,* and *A Midsummer's Night Dream*, to name but a few. He was born at Stratford-Upon-Avon in 1564, and married Anne Hathaway who also lived in the region.

Daniel Defoe (1660 – 1731)

He is best known for his story of the shipwrecked Robinson Crusoe, written in 1719. It tells the tale of the survival of a marooned mariner, stranded on a remote island off the coast of Venezuela for 28 years, and his meeting up with Man Friday, a native cannibal Indian, who becomes his companion and servant.

Sir Walter Scott (1771 – 1832)

Sir Walter Scott was a Scottish baronet and famous author who contributed to both English and Scottish literature in his works, such as *Ivanhoe* and *Rob Roy.* Besides being a celebrated author, he was, by profession, an advocate judge and legal administrator. His book *Ivanhoe* is set in medieval England in the 12th century, and *Rob Roy* is set in the period just before the 1715 Jacobite uprising, when Scotland was in much turmoil.

Jane Austen (1775 – 1817)

A very famous English novelist who wrote books confined to middle-class provincial society. Her works, like *Sense and Sensibility* and *Pride and Prejudice*, are popular even today, and have been made into films and TV adaptations. She showed great skill in drawing her characters and situations with a certain irony.

Charles Dickens (1812 – 1870)

Dickens was one of the most famous and popular of English authors. He wrote about the poverty, harshness, and social evils of Victorian England in books like *Oliver Twist, David Copperfield,* and *Great Expectations*. His characters were very memorable, like Fagin in Oliver Twist, Mr. Micawber in David Copperfield, and Miss. Havisham in Great Expectations. Most of the characters he 'painted' had strange personalities and even stranger names. Almost all his books have been made into films and TV adaptations. In many of his works, he focuses on the ill-treatment of children, and the harshness metered out to them. He is probably one of the most popular Victorian writers to this day.

The Brönte Sisters (1816 – 1855)

The two most famous of the Brönte sisters were Charlotte and her sister Emily. They were the daughters of a clergyman, and lived in the Parsonage in Haworth, West Yorkshire, with their father, sister Anne, and brother Branwell. They took to writing as a pastime, and Charlotte produced her first work, *Jane Eyre,* in 1847, and Emily wrote *Wuthering Heights* in the same year. Anne also followed in the family tradition and produced a book, *The Tenant of Wildfell Hall,* a year later. The works of all three sisters became very well-known, and have been made into films and TV dramas.

Mark Twain (1833 – 1910)

Who doesn't love the lively characters of Tom Sawyer and Huckleberry Finn?—Creations of the famous American author, Mark Twain. His real name was Samuel Langhorne Clemens, but he wrote under the pen name of Mark Twain. *Tom Sawyer* and *The Adventures of Huckleberry Finn* are among the most famous of American literature, and are set along the Mississippi River. Their adventures include encounters with Injun Joe, and involve buried treasure in a cave. Mark Twain also wrote *The Prince and the Pauper*, set in England in the time of King Henry VIII, where his son, Prince Edward, gets involved with a look-alike pauper boy, and they exchange roles, which leads to an interesting and confusing situation.

Robert Louis Stevenson (1850 – 1894)

He wrote adventure stories like *Kidnapped* and *Treasure Island*, as also *The Strange Case of Dr. Jekyll and Mr. Hyde*. For the sake of his health, he travelled widely in the Pacific region, visiting places like Hawaii, and other islands in the South Seas. He finally settled on the island of Samoa where he died in 1894.

Rudyard Kipling (1865 – 1936)

This eminent author was born in India in 1865 where he wrote most of his stories, like *Kim* and *The Jungle Book*, the most loved of his stories written mainly for children. Among his other works were *Gunga Din* and *Plain Tales from the Hills*. He was considered an 'Anglo-Indian'—the term used in the 19th century for people of British origin being born and settling in India (then part of the British Empire). He travelled widely in his later years, visiting countries like the United States and South Africa. He died in England in 1936.

Throughout the ages, Art, Music, and Literature have been the centrepiece of our cultural heritage, without which our lives would have been very dull and boring indeed.

Commerce, Trade, and Industry

Throughout much of recorded history, humans have always been traders, exchanging goods with their neighbours. Before the invention of money, goods were bartered by our ancient ancestors, and this trading helped greatly with human communication and contact. Prehistoric commercial routes between Northern and Southern Europe were established to transport amber, a rare and much prized substance, and then the Silk Route was established, which was not only a trading but also a cultural link between the West and the East. This route was used by traders, merchants, pilgrims, and suchlike to travel from China to the Mediterranean Sea. The Romans, too, established overland trade routes to India to import silks in exchange for their precious silver and gold.

Besides overland trade routes, civilizations like the ancient Phoenicians used shipping passages to transport goods and merchandise around the Mediterranean area. Seafaring nations with their navigational skills had a great advantage, and the Portuguese soon established a sea route to India and the Spice Islands for the very profitable spice trade. The British were also great seafarers, and soon established links with Asia and set up the East India Company for very valuable trade with India. They also established links with China for the highly profitable, but nefarious, trade in exporting opium, grown in India, to that country, which inevitably led to the opium wars. Then later, in the 1800s, tea growing was started in the Himalayan regions, and the lucrative trade in tea commenced, with especially fast boats called tea clippers, like the Cutty Sark, being built to facilitate this trade.

Going back to Elizabethan times, adventurers and explorers like Sir Walter Raleigh introduced tobacco to the British Isles from America, and this led to the fashion of smoking, and the lucrative tobacco trade, which today is frowned upon. At about the same time, the potato—found in South America—was introduced to Europe by the Spanish, as also the tomato. This, along with other plants, like the chilli, greatly improved the diet and flavour of food in Europe, and spread to the rest of the world.

The cotton and the sugar trade were also very important commercial imports, and soon the cotton mills of Lancashire were busy with the weaving of cotton and linen, while the Tate & Lyle factories refined cane sugar. Cotton was extensively grown in India, which was then a British Colony, brought back to England, turned into cloth, and then re-exported back into India as the finished product. During the Industrial Revolution, Britain became the hub of a great manufacturing plant, importing raw materials from her colonies, turning them into finished products, and then re-exporting them around the globe, and thus became a prosperous nation.

Up to the middle of the 20th century, Britain was one of the leading manufacturing countries in the world. The 'Made in England' logo ensured the quality of its products from razor blades to motor cars. Factories mushroomed everywhere, their smoke-stacks billowing out smoke and fumes. The labour force, which had hitherto been employed mainly as farm labourers and domestic servants, quickly sought employment in factories and manufacturing plants, where the wages were more rewarding. But competition was building up elsewhere in the world, particularly in the United States, as Europe was still teetering with the aftermath of the Second World War.

However, it did not take long for other nations to catch up. With the loss of its colonies in Asia and Africa, Britain took a lesser and lesser role in world manufacture, and countries like West Germany and Japan, propped up by finance from the United States, became greater players in the Industrial World. India, hitherto one of the greatest importers of British goods, gained independence and curtailed their imports from the rest of the world, and instead relied on their indigenous manufactures.

The motor car industry, hitherto dominated by the USA and Great Britain, began to be overtaken by Japan in the second half of the twentieth century, to dominate the market by producing cheap and reliable cars. The same went for the electronics industry, and huge Japanese giants like Sony dominated the market. As a result, both the motor industry and the electronics industry, among others, have dwindled in the United Kingdom and are also having an adverse effect on the American car giants, like Ford and GMC.

Businesses have always looked around the world for places where labour rates are low, and today China is one of the largest manufacturing countries in the world, and the 'Made in

China' label is appearing on more and more products, particularly electronics.

In this Global Economy, it is becoming increasingly difficult to identify where a product originates, for although it may have a familiar brand name that would indicate it was, for example, a British product, it may well have been manufactured in a completely different country.

The transportation of goods around the world in huge ocean-going container ships, and large cargo planes, have made it possible to move a vast range of goods and products all over the world with an ease that could only be dreamt of by our ancient ancestors. Foodstuffs, like fresh fruit and vegetables, can be transported across the globe and be available in your local supermarket or high street shop in a matter of days. You could be eating an orange that came from Spain, Israel, or South Africa, and no matter where it came from, it would still taste just as fresh.

With the formation of the European Union in the 1950s, it has expanded from 6 original member states to 28, and now includes some countries like Poland, Hungary, and the Czech Republic which were formerly part of the Soviet Union. This Common Market has greatly facilitated trade and the movement of labour within the EU. Also, with a single currency—the Euro (adopted by most of the EU member states)—the movement of money and currency transactions, as well as travel, have been made that much easier. Great Britain, who joined the EU in 1973, however, is somewhat at odds with the rest of the Community and has stuck to its original currency, the pound. There is some apprehension in Great Britain about its membership, and the influx of immigrants from other EU countries, like Poland, Romania, and Bulgaria. Great Britain had always played a dominant role in trade, and some of the dictates that now come from Europe are a difficult pill to swallow. However, rules are rules, and if one desires to be part of a club, they should be followed. At the time of writing, Britain is dithering about whether it should break away from Europe and perhaps re-establish closer trading links with its former colonies, like India, Australia, New Zealand, and Canada. Whether this would be a beneficial decision is a moot point, as the pros and cons have to be considered. On the one hand we would save the costs of EU membership which is £15bn gross (0.06% of GDP) or £6.883 billion net; on the other, Britain would swiftly have to negotiate bilateral deals with dozens of countries. However, Britain has always been a successful trading nation, and no doubt it would survive outside the shackles of the EU.

Science and Technology

Astronomy

We do not have to go back very far in history to establish when scientific thought first began, merely to about 500 years ago, when early astronomers started to study and wonder about the movements of planets against the background of stars. It was originally thought that the Earth was the centre of the Universe, and that the Sun, Moon, and planets revolved around it. Only with the study of the movement of planets did Nicholas Copernicus in the mid-1500s conclude that it was not the Sun that revolved around the Earth, but the other way about—the Earth and all the planets orbited around the Sun. Italian astronomer Galileo Galilei picked up this idea, and devised an instrument called a telescope, through which he studied the motion of the moons that revolved around the planet Jupiter, in an effort to prove his model of the Solar System. This new idea of the Earth not being centre stage to the Universe was considered heretical by the established Church, and Galileo's ideas were quickly quashed by threat of arrest and torture.

However, his model of the Solar System was taken up by Sir Isaac Newton in the mid-1600s and he not only confirmed Galileo's theories, but also conceived the theory of gravity, which was a force that caused objects to fall back to Earth, and held the Solar System together. As such, Newton became one of the great pioneers of scientific thought, and many of his theories still hold good to this day.

Other great astronomers, such as William Herschel, followed in the footsteps of Newton. He discovered the planet Uranus, and made the largest telescope in his day, though it was an unwieldy instrument and of poor optical quality. Another famous astronomer was Charles Messier, a Frenchman who published a catalogue of fuzzy star-like objects in 1774, known as Messier objects. He gave these M numbers for objects like the Crab Nebular (M1) and the great Orion Nebula (M42), and these classifications are still used to this day.

However, it was not until the 20th century that astronomy and astrophysics really got under way, with astrophysicists like Albert Einstein, whose theories of Relativity changed the scientific world, and whose famous equation of $E=mc^2$ helped unleash the power of the atom which resulted in the creation of the first nuclear bomb. Then Edwin Hubble came on the scene, and his identification of galaxies outside our own was a breakthrough, and changed our concept of the Universe forever.

Today, huge telescopes are sited across the globe, we can peer into the heavens at higher and higher magnifications, and the beauties and wonders of the Universe are being revealed. We even have the Hubble Space Telescope in outer space, whose photographs are of the utmost clarity, because it does not have the disadvantage of peering through the Earth's atmosphere, as all Earth-bound telescopes have to do.

Mathematics

In ancient times, the Egyptians and Babylonians used methods of calculation from as far back as 1900 B.C., in the construction of their great building projects. However, the study of mathematics as a subject in its own right began in about the 6th century B.C., with Pythagoras, a Greek philosopher and mathematician, who was responsible for the Pythagorean Theorem—'the square of the hypotenuse is equal to the sum of the squares of the other two sides'—which is familiar to all schoolchildren. Other Greek philosophers like Plato and Euclid, also played an important role in the development of mathematics, and Euclid is often referred to as 'The Father of Geometry'. Adoption of the Hindu-Arabic numerical system was also vital, as with the old Roman numerical system it was impossible to make calculations. However, bursts of mathematical inspiration were often followed by centuries of stagnation, particularly through the Dark Ages, when scientific thought throughout Europe was suppressed by the Church.

The 17th century saw an unprecedented explosion of mathematical and scientific ideas across Europe by astronomers like Galileo Galilei, Tycho Brahe, and Johannes Kepler, in their efforts to calculate planetary motions. Sir Isaac Newton also discovered the laws of physics, explaining Kepler's laws on planetary motion. Gottfried Wilhelm Leibniz, who was arguably one of the most important mathematicians of the 17th century, developed calculus, and much of his calculus notation is still in use today. Great scientific geniuses like Albert Einstein also mathematically proved many of his scientific theories, such as the bending of light under extreme gravitational forces.

As all school kids who have sweated over their arithmetic, algebra, geometry, trigonometry, etc., will know, mathematics is a very complex subject, unless you have an aptitude towards it, and some may never need it much in their later lives unless they aspire to be an astrophysicist or nuclear scientist.

High mathematics, however, are in use today to work out complex calculations involved in space travel and exploration, and, albeit with the help of powerful computers, can calculate trajectories of spacecraft and land robotic vehicles on planets like Mars to within a few feet. Without mathematics, all this would have been impossible.

Metallurgy

The earliest recorded metal employed by humans appears to be gold, from which trinkets and ornaments were made. Silver, copper, tin, and iron were also discovered by our ancient ancestors, allowing a limited amount of metal-working.

However, soon our ancient ancestors made certain technical advances in the forging of metals to make tools and weapons, though this was done on a more practical basis rather than a scientific one. As far back as 3000 B.C., the ancient Egyptians were producing bronze—an alloy of copper and tin. But this metal was not hard enough to be of much use for efficient weapons and tools, and it was only between 1200

B.C. and 1000 B.C. that the forging of iron began, which led to the fabrication of steel (a combination of iron and carbon), which was the ideal metal, due to its lighter weight and tensile strength, and its ability to hold the sharpness of a blade.

Since then, metals have played a significant role in bringing us out of the Stone Age into a highly developed society. The inclusion of metals such as aluminium, chromium, copper, magnesium, nickel, zinc, and titanium—often used as alloys (a combination of two or more metals), have enabled us to make most of the products for our everyday use and weaponry. Also, these are available in abundance, and with specialised mining techniques to extract them from the earth, huge mining projects started across the globe, and continue to this day.

Chemistry

In early times, our knowledge and understanding of the elements that surround us was very limited. Early Greek philosophers, going back to 450 B.C., reckoned that there were only four elements in nature—earth, air, fire, and water. We now know that there are 92 elements that occur naturally. An element is a substance that occurs in nature, and is not made up from anything else. They are the basic ingredients from which everything else is made. Metals, like gold, silver, iron, lead, and copper are some of the many elements that are found on Earth.

But going back in history, early attempts at chemistry were dominated by alchemy, and in their search for making gold from such things as lead and copper, alchemists in their dabbling, accidentally discovered many new chemicals and techniques, such as sublimation and distillation. This has been the case for many accidental chemical discoveries; you search for one thing, but discover something completely different.

For instance, the finding of the first chemical element, Phosphorus, was discovered by a bankrupt German merchant, Henning Brand in 1649, who in his efforts to discover the Philosopher's Stone—a mythical object that was supposed to turn inexpensive base metals into gold—experimented with distilled human urine which resulted in a glowing white substance, which he named Phosphorus. But he kept this discovery secret until 1680, when Robert Boyle rediscovered this element and published his findings.

Another example: William Henry Perkin, an English chemist (when he was only 18 years old), while trying to create a synthetic version of quinine, an anti-malaria drug, discovered that the gooey black mess at the bottom of his flask when mixed with alcohol turned a brilliant purple colour. Purely by accident, he discovered the first aniline dye, which he called Mauvine. Since this discovery in 1856, dyes made from aniline, a by-product of coal-tar, have been used in paints and dyes from that day onwards.

However, it was not understood how atoms bonded with other atoms to create chemical compounds, and things like the air that we breathe and the water that we drink were not fully comprehended.

Eventually, in the continuation of chemists to persevere in their experiments, many of the familiar elements around us were identified, and a table (the Periodic Table) was drawn up and published in 1869 by Dmitri Mendeleev, a Russian chemist, who built upon earlier discoveries of elements by other scientists. This table of elements was continuously added to for over a century to include all the 92 different elements that we know today.

In 1907, a breakthrough in the development of synthetic materials took place with the invention of Bakelite. This was one of the first plastics made from synthetic components. Bakelite was widely used for its electrical non-conductivity and heat-resistant properties in electrical insulators, radio and telephone casings, and for such diverse products as kitchenware and jewellery. Bakelite was largely replaced when Plastics were invented and introduced in the 1940s and '50s, and today, plastic and its derivatives, such as Polystyrene, Nylon, Synthetic Rubber, etc., is so widely used that it forms almost all the products in use today. These materials are so versatile that they can be moulded into any shape, cheaply and easily, given any colour, and take on any form—from rigid structures to flexible ones, and can be woven into fabrics.

Medicine

The practice of medicine for the treatment of our ills goes back to antiquity. In ancient times, priests, shamans, witch doctors, and medicine men, used herbs, animal parts, and minerals for the treatment of human illnesses. In later times, physicians appeared on the scene, and perhaps the most famous of all was the ancient Greek physician, Hippocrates, who is revered as the 'father of western medicine', and whose Hippocratic Oath became the medical ethic for all medical practitioners to follow.

However, disease was not fully understood, and when the plague ravaged Europe in the 14th and 15th centuries, the people at that time had no inkling that the disease was spread by fleas that infested rats. All they knew was that their family and friends were dying all around them, and whole villages and communities were being wiped out by some terrible pestilence.

The treatment of diseases and other ailments, metered out by attendant physicians, was often so drastic that the patient probably suffered more pain and discomfort from the treatment than from the ailment or disease itself. For instance, in the 17th century, syphilis was often treated with mercury, a very poisonous substance, and the side-effects could be painful and terrifying. In many cases, the patient died from significant mercury poisoning.

It was only in the 19th century, and beyond, that advances in chemistry and the identification of bacteria and viruses meant that true advances in medicine had begun. With the introduction of antiseptics and anaesthesia in the performance of operations, the prospects of a patient surviving the amputation of a limb greatly improved. Hitherto, the patient was given a piece of leather to bite on while the surgeon sawed off his leg—hence the term of 'saw-bones' for a surgeon, and when infection set in, through the use of dirty medical instruments and a lack of hand washing, the fate of the patient was usually sealed. However, with the discovery of Penicillin, the first antibiotic, survival rates were increased a hundred-fold.

Actually, Penicillin was another accidental discovery. When Alexander Fleming, in 1928, discovered some of his petri dishes with cultures of a staphylococci bacteria had been contaminated by a fungus, he was about to throw these away, but when he by chance looked at the specimens under his microscope, he found that the fungus had completely destroyed the bacteria, and thus was Penicillin, the wonder drug, discovered!

Vaccination was another medical breakthrough in the prevention of diseases like smallpox, a contagious and very deadly disease. Whereas previously this terrible disease accounted for the deaths of 300 million people in the 20th century alone, thankfully, this dreadful scourge has now been completely eliminated by mass vaccination. It is through the work of chemists and microbiologists, like Louis Pasteur, that other deadly diseases, such as rabies and anthrax, can be prevented, resulting in a great saving of life.

With modern-day medicine, many of the diseases that afflicted us are now treatable. Also, great strides have been made in surgical techniques, and it is now quite usual to have one of our organs replaced by a transplant. The use of x-rays, scanners, and other sophisticated medical equipment has been vital in identifying medical conditions. All in all, we humans enjoy a longer and healthier life than our ancestors, thanks to all the advances made by modern medicine.

Transport

One can say that one of the first technical advances our ancestors made in transport was the invention of the wheel. At first these were clumsy affairs, with two semicircles of solid wood joined together by two other pieces of wood, but later these primitive wheels developed into more sophisticated ones with spokes, such as those used on Egyptian chariots. These sorts of spoke-wheels continued well into the 20th century, until they were overtaken by wheels with pneumatic tyres, which are used on our modern-day motor vehicles. Further developments took place with the invention of springs and shock-absorbers to make the ride more comfortable and reduce or eliminate the jolts that occurred whenever a bump or rut in the road was encountered.

Travel was a slow and uncomfortable progression over many days, weeks, or months for our predecessors in their efforts to travel from one place to another, whether this was by road or sea, with only muscle or wind power to drive their vehicles and vessels, and this went on for thousands of years. It was only with the invention of the steam locomotive in 1825 by George Stephenson that travel at last became quicker and more comfortable for would-be passengers. The first railway was the Stockton and Darlington Railway, and then the Liverpool and Manchester Railway was opened in 1830 for both passenger and freight trains. Since then, railway networks have crossed the continents with faster and more powerful engines, powered by diesel and electric motors.

However, we humans had always looked at birds with envy at their ease of travel through the air, as it was by far an easier, quicker, and more direct means of transportation, avoiding the obstacles encountered by travelling over terrain or rough and unfriendly seas. Even Leonardo da Vinci, way back in the 15th century, attempted to design a flying machine.

The challenge of travelling through the skies was met first by hot-air balloons and then airships—huge torpedo-shaped gas balloons, fitted with a gondola for carrying passengers, and propellers to drive the craft through the air. This mode of transport began in the early part of the 20th century, but this means of travel was abandoned after the Hindenburg disaster in 1937, when the airship burst into flames and crashed as it approached its mooring mast at Lakehurst, New Jersey, on its arrival from Germany. This caused the death of many passengers and aircrew, and shattered public confidence in airships from that day onwards, resulting in its abandonment as a safe means of air travel. The main problem with these gas-filled craft was the envelope filled with highly flammable hydrogen gas, and it was not until helium was used instead that modern-day airships were used in a limited fashion, though not as a means of travel.

Meanwhile, in the early 1900s, the Wright brothers, Orville and Wilbur, were inventing and building the world's first successful aeroplane, the Kitty Hawk. Although this aircraft only flew for a few yards and just about left the ground, it was still considered the first manned flight through the air, and won the two brothers a place in history.

Another great milestone in aviation was the historic flight of Charles Lindbergh, when he flew across the Atlantic in 1927 in his monoplane, The Spirit of St. Louis, making the flight from New York to Paris in 33½ hours. This greatly increased public confidence in the aeroplane as a means of travelling through the air.

From then on, engineers, designers, and inventors continued to improve on earlier aircraft design throughout the 20th century, to produce faster and faster aircraft. Finally, with the development of the jet engine, the slower propeller driven passenger aircraft were replaced by jet airliners, and today one can travel over the continents, and indeed the world, in a matter of hours, instead of months and even years. We have literally leaped from Kitty Hawk to Concorde in less than 70 years.

Communications

Apart from the spoken word, written communication was largely done in early times by scribes and priests, who wrote or copied passages of text by hand. Monks in churches and monasteries did this for early transcriptions of the Bible and Biblical texts. It was only with the advent of printing, by Johannes Gutenberg in the mid-1400s, that pages, with characters and illustrations, could be printed and bound into books. This greatly spread communication, because now multiple copies could be made available and published for others to read. This is how Galileo spread his theories of scientific ideas on planetary motions round the Sun, which eventually led to his books being banned by the Church and his consequent trial and arrest.

The task of conveying messages in our early history was done by sending written messages via a courier, who had to sometimes brave the battlefield to deliver the vital message to the recipient. He had to travel as fast as possible, and this was often done on horseback, the quickest means of transportation at the time. In America in the 1860s, a mail delivery system was established, called the Pony Express, which delivered letters and small packages from St. Joseph, Missouri, across the Great Plains, over the Rocky Mountains and the Sierra Nevada to Sacramento in California, by riders on horseback, using a series of relay stations to change rider and horse. With the introduction of stamped postal services, like the Royal Mail (beginning in 1840 in England and 1847 in the U.S.), letters and parcels could be delivered to their destinations anywhere in the world. However, this was still a slow process, and a faster means of communication was still very necessary. This was met by the introduction of the telegraph in the 1840s, which was a means of instant communication between the sender and receiver, using a series of coded electrical signals through a telegraph wire.

In the second-half of the 19th century, an undersea cable was laid to connect Great Britain to North America, which was an enormous project and completed at great cost. The first attempts at direct communication between the two countries were largely unsuccessful, but eventually the transmission of the signal was improved and telegraphic transmissions could be made. This undersea cabling was extended to cover some other parts of the world, and greatly improved the transmission, particularly of news, between the continents.

Telephones, first introduced in the 1870s by the Bell Company in America, became the main and most popular means of communication between businesses and households. Here one could pick up the phone and talk to a member of family or a friend instantly, and sometimes the urgent pealing of the telephone interrupted a conversation, and one broke off to pick up the telephone, which is a habit that still persists to this day.

However, it was not possible for ships to use the telegraph or telephone as these required wires to connect them. They still had to resort to visual signals, such as flags using a system called Semaphore to convey their messages, and light signals using a series of flashes to represent the dots (short) and dashes (long) used in Morse Code that represented the different characters in the alphabet, as used for the telegraph. It was not until the advent of radio in the early 1900s that wireless telegraphy could be used as a form of communication, which dispensed with the need for wires.

Whereas in the past communication had to rely on handwritten letters and messages to be delivered, sometimes between continents, which could take several months over sea or land, with the advent of radio—accredited to Gugliemo Marconi, an Italian inventor—wireless messages could be broadcast over land or sea instantly, using a device called a radio. Not only could code signals be broadcast this way, but eventually the human voice and music.

Early radio sets were primitive appliances when first introduced, as they required a crystal to receive the signal, and headphones to hear the faint sound. When valves, made of glass tubes, were introduced to amplify the signal, real progress could be made, and radio sets began to be found in every household, where families tuned in every evening to sit around the radio and listen to their favourite radio program, broadcast by the many radio stations that abounded, both locally and around the world.

Television soon followed in the 1950s, and now one was not only able to hear one's favourite program, but to view it on the television screen, made from a cathode ray tube. However, there was a problem with television signals, because unlike short-wave radio signals, they could not be bounced off the ionosphere and broadcast around the globe. As a consequence, relay stations had to be built so that these signals could be picked up and re-transmitted. It was not until the introduction of satellites, that signals could be picked up in outer space and re-transmitted over the world. The first International television program broadcast between Britain and North America took place in 1962.

The great breakthrough in electronics took place in the mid-1950s with the invention and introduction of the transistor. This tiny device was made from a silicon chip, and soon replaced the cumbersome and energy-consuming valves, so radios could be made small, compact, and portable. They could be powered by a few dry-cell batteries, as they did not need much power to operate them. This evolved into the integrated circuit, or microchip, where hundreds, thousands, and now billions of transistors can be incorporated into a single chip, sometimes as small as your fingernail.

Flat display screens, like Plasma and LCD, were a great innovation, as now images could be displayed on portable devices like digital cameras, computers, and hand-held devices, such as tablets and cell phones. This did away with the cumbersome cathode-ray tube, which consumed a lot of power and was bulky and heavy.

With these developments in electronics and the introduction of the Internet in the 1990s, communication became instantaneous, and we can now interconnect with each other, or indeed the world, by speaking or typing messages on our cell-phones, computers, or tablets. Social

Media systems, like Facebook and Twitter, were also established, and groups of friends can instantly intercommunicate with each other. It is also possible now to communicate visually with someone across the world by using systems like Skype and Facetime.

Energy

In ancient times, the only energy source available to our cave-man ancestors was the burning of wood to produce warmth and light. This energy was also used to prepare cooked food. Later, the heat from fire was used to melt and forge metals to make into tools and weapons. So fire was our first form of energy.

However, throughout most of history, a source of power was lacking, as it was only muscle power, wind, and water that were used to drive whatever machinery we devised. For centuries, we travelled around in ships powered only by the wind, and used horses and cattle to draw our carriages and wagons right until the middle of the 1800s, until the steam locomotive was invented by George Stephenson in 1825. Yet we managed to travel around the world, plough our fields, and grind our corn using only these primitive sources of power, which is a credit to our forefathers.

With the advent of the steam engine, we humans at last discovered a means of using steam-powered machines to drive our machinery and replace the horse and carriage for transportation of passengers and goods. However, it was not

131

until the discovery and use of electricity that we really began to make progress and develop into a modern-day society as we have today.

Electricity has been with us since the dawn of time, although it was not recognised by us humans as such. Electric storms have lit up our skies with lightning, and our human body uses electricity that passes through the nerves in our eyes, hearts, brains, and muscles. Some types of fish, such as electric eels and torpedo fish, have been using electricity from the time of their evolution to stun their prey, and can give you a shock of several volts should you happen to touch them. It was by studying these electrical fish that led to the invention of the first battery.

The ancient Romans became aware of electricity when they rubbed a piece of amber against wool, and this induced a mysterious force that attracted small particles of light objects like hair or dust to stick to it. You can see this effect quite easily by running a comb through your hair, then placing it close to a tiny scrap of paper.

However, this form of static electricity was not of much use, and though used as a novelty and source of entertainment by early experimenters, it was not until the flow of an electric current was developed that we could usefully employ this source of power. An electric current is produced by the flow of electrons—sub-atomic particles—through copper wires to the equipment it is connected to, be it a light-bulb or an electric motor. It is *the* source of power that is used today to work just about everything, from your electric toaster to your home computer. Without it, our modern-day world would come to a grinding halt, as we have become so dependent on its use that it is now virtually indispensable. Just try doing without your electricity for a day! Your whole household would practically come to a stop. Yet, our ancestors managed to get along without this energy source for thousands and thousands of years.

We owe a debt of gratitude to the great achievements of scientists and inventors like André Ampere, George Simon Ohm, Alessandro Volta, and Michael Faraday, for our understanding and use of electricity, as also Thomas Edison for bringing us the light-bulb, which truly lit up our world.

Other sources of energy produced by the burning of fossil fuels have been used in the more recent past, such as the combustion gasoline engine, which has been with us since the early 1900s to power and drive our cars. We have not yet found a suitable alternative. Electricity to power motor vehicles is in limited use, as they rely on batteries for the power source, and these are not yet efficient enough to drive our vehicles very far before they need recharging. Hybrid cars, which use a mixture of the two technologies, are becoming increasingly popular. Our aeroplanes also still have to use fossil fuels in the form of aviation fuel. Even our ships have to be fuelled by diesel engines, using another fossil fuel.

Gas was another useful energy source, and is still being used to heat our homes and cook our food. In the beginning of the 19th century, gas lighting was installed in homes to replace the use of candles, and was also used for street lighting. But this was superseded by electric light. Gas was formerly manufactured by purifying coal-gas, but this was overtaken in the 1970s when natural gas resources were found under England's coastal waters, which led to the building of massive gas platforms in places like the North Sea to tap this valuable resource.

However, since the detonation of the Atom bomb over Hiroshima and Nagasaki in 1945, the awesome power of the atom was released, bringing us into the Atomic Age. This new form of energy can be harnessed in nuclear reactors and used as a heat source to replace coal-fired furnaces. These nuclear reactors are used in power stations to heat water and produce steam to drive our electric generators. So in the end we come back to electricity. We have not yet been able to use the power of the atom for anything else, but the development of nuclear-fusion reactors in the distant future is a possibility for a new energy source, which we desperately need to replace the use of fossil fuels. New technologies are also being developed using such things as solar and wind power, and biomass energy.

Computing & Electronics

Throughout the ages, people have used calculating machines to help work out their sums. One of the very earliest devices was the abacus—rows of beads threaded through wires on a frame. The use of the abacus in ancient China goes back to the 2nd century B.C. Calculating machines, like the comptometer, using a series of keys, was introduced in 1887 to perform arithmetical calculations, and mechanical calculators such as adding machines, and even cash registers, were used right up to the middle of the 1970s when they were overtaken by the electronic calculator, which could be carried conveniently in your pocket.

However, the first electronic computer was conceived by the little-known and largely uncredited Tommy Flowers, working at the Post Office Research Station in the 1930s when he was exploring the possibility of using electronics for the telephone exchange. He was soon commissioned to design and build the Colossus machine for Bletchley Park to break the encrypted signals of the German Enigma machine in 1944. Colossus was the world's first electronic digital and programmable computer. It used a huge array of valves, giving off an enormous amount of heat, and used paper-tape as a means of inputting data.

Early computers had fixed programs, and changing its function required hard re-wiring, usually done by hand, to reprogram the machine. This was replaced in time by the stored-program computer, which could receive a set of instructions and hold it in memory. The earlier computing machines generally used punch-cards or paper tape as input for the data, but this was later replaced by magnetic tapes and disks. However, great improvements took place when the earlier valves were replaced by energy-efficient and space-saving transistors, and later the microchip.

However, early computers were very large machines with an array of peripherals, and were only suitable for businesses where sufficient space and environmental conditions were available. Such large and powerful machines are still in use today in business and military establishments.

Day by day, month by month, and year by year, computers are playing a more and more dominant role in our everyday lives and experience. Whereas in the days of their early introduction, they were often looked upon with suspicion and scepticism, today they are depended on more and more. Computers have developed from mere calculating machines into machines that can use voice recognition to convert speech to text and vice-versa, obey vocal commands, optically read handwriting, scan bar-codes, and are connected to every ATM machine and credit card reader in the country. Now-a-days, you hardly exist unless your records are held on a computer somewhere. All commerce would cease instantly if all computers crashed simultaneously. This is not impossible, as strong magnetic fields emitted by massive solar flares could generate radiation that would frazzle the delicate electronics that computers rely on. This is a far more likely scenario than an asteroid or comet suddenly impacting with the planet—a doomsday apocalypse that science programs on TV love to dwell on!

The introduction of the home computer in 1977 brought the computer into our everyday human experience. One of the first to be introduced was the Sinclair ZX Spectrum, which used a cassette tape deck to input the data and your television screen as a display monitor. The keyboard and processor came as a single plug-in unit. However, the software industry had not yet got underway, and the programming of the machine was left to the owner. In a matter of a few years, however, both the hardware and software industry mushroomed and more and more powerful machines were introduced, using a huge variety of software that had become available on the market. The laptop computer and tablet are now in such common use that it is rare for a household to be found without any of these devices. With the introduction of the Internet, the whole world is now virtually at our fingertips.

Among the other electronic wizardry that surrounds us today, are our cell phones, GPS navigational devices, our pocket calculators, our tablets—where one can carry hundreds of volumes of books in a single device—as also our entire music collection held on our iPods. With smart-phones, most or all of these devices, including a camera, can be incorporated into one single unit. All this is possible by the invention of the microprocessor held on a tiny silicone chip.

However, one has to wonder whether all these new gadgets are making us into a more introverted society. These days when you travel on the train, everyone is staring at their cell phone or iPad instead of interacting with someone else, or simply looking out of the window and enjoying the scenery. Conversing with our fellow humans has always been an important development in our culture, and social-intercourse is something that we would not want to lose.

Space Exploration

Travelling in outer space would be impossible without the rocket. Other propulsion systems like the jet engine and the propeller are useless, as they rely on air to work, and of course, there is no air in outer space! It was the ancient Chinese in the 13th century who made the first rockets, filling a tube with gunpowder—which they also invented—and lighting it so that it rose into the sky with a shower of sparks. We still use these sorts of rockets in our firework displays.

However, it was not until the beginning of the 20th century that travelling in outer space was inspired by such writers as Jules Verne and H.G. Wells, and scientists considered that the rocket was the only engine that was capable of leaving Earth's atmosphere and travelling in space. In 1912, Robert Goddard began a serious analysis of rocket technology, and his early experiments led to the development of the first liquid-fuelled rocket in 1926, which when tested, reached a considerable altitude, though not of course, leaving the Earth's atmosphere.

It was only in 1943, when the Germans developed the V-2 rocket as a weapon of war, that the first truly successful rockets were introduced. They could fly high into the atmosphere and reach London from Peenemünde in Germany (from where they were launched), to wreak havoc in the city with the high explosives they carried in their warheads.

After the end of World War II, the German scientists who had been engaged in developing rocket technology, like Wernher von Braun, were divided up between the victorious nations such as the United States and the Soviet Union, where they were given the facilities to further engage in the development of rocket technology.

This led to a spectacular feat on October 4th 1957, with the successful launch into outer space of the first satellite, Sputnik 1, by the Russians. This came as a complete shock to the Americans who were largely unsuccessful in developing a rocket capable of leaving the Earth's atmosphere—their various attempts all having failed. So the Space Race began in earnest.

The Russians launched the first man into space, Yuri Gagarin, in the Vostok spacecraft on 12th April 1961, and clearly the Americans had a lot of catching up to do. But they were hot on the heels of the Soviets, and only a month later, had put their first astronaut, Alan Shepard, into a sub-orbital flight using the Mercury-Redstone 3 rocket, the first successful one the Americans had developed.

But it was reaching the Moon that was the first goal in the Space Race. The Russians had successfully impacted a spacecraft, Lunar 2, on the surface of the Moon on 13th September 1959, which was the first craft ever to have reached the Moon. The Americans followed this with their

Ranger 4 spacecraft in 1962. The Russians were also the first to send a spacecraft, Lunar 3, around the Moon to photograph the other side, which gave us the first sightings of the Moon's surface (this is always hidden from us, as we are only able to see one side of the Moon from Earth). They were also able to successfully land an unmanned spacecraft, Lunar 9, on the surface of the Moon on 3rd February 1966.

Of course, there had been several failures in these early Russian attempts, but whereas the USSR always hailed their successes, they kept very silent about their failures.

However, with President Kennedy's promise on May 25, 1961 of 'landing a man on the Moon and returning him safely to the Earth' by the end of the 1960s, the Americans began the Apollo Program in 1968 to achieve this goal. A massive rocket, the Saturn V booster, was developed, and was the most powerful rocket ever to have been made, and could carry a crew of three in the Command Module. The Service Module with one rocket attached, and the Moon Lander, comprised the rest of the spacecraft for its onward voyage to the Moon.

In order to achieve escape-velocity from the Earth's gravity, a speed of at least 7 miles a second had to be reached. This couldn't be done by only a single rocket, so the answer—proposed by Wernher von Braun—was to build the rocket in three stages; stage 1 would carry the rocket so far into the atmosphere, where it would detach and fall off; stage 2 would then take over. This too would be ejected, and the rocket of stage 3 would carry it into outer space. This could be shut off when the required speed was reached, as the rest of the journey throughout space would not require any further power, and the craft could continue on its way forever through outer space in perpetual motion.

However, the Apollo Project met with its first disaster on January 27, 1967. When training for a manned flight, astronauts Grissom, White, and Chaffee, while testing the spacecraft, were all tragically killed when an electrical fire began in the cabin. Because it was filled with a 100% pure oxygen atmosphere at high pressure, the fire spread so rapidly that the astronauts did not have a chance of opening the hatch and escaping. Thereafter, the atmosphere in the cabin for future flights was changed to a mixture of oxygen and nitrogen gas.

Despite this setback, the Apollo Project continued, and in December 1968, astronauts Frank Borman, James Lovell, and William Anders made the first manned journey to the Moon. The mission wasn't designed to land on the surface, but merely to orbit the Moon and then return to Earth. The Apollo 8 mission completed 10 orbits of the Moon before returning the astronauts safely back to Earth.

Re-entry into the Earth's atmosphere was perhaps the most hazardous part of the journey, as the spacecraft was travelling at incredible speed. All parts of the remaining spacecraft were jettisoned and only the capsule returned to Earth. When it encountered the Earth's atmosphere, it approached at a critical attitude and angle where the heat-shield which protected the capsule took the brunt of the fiery flames that engulfed it. When the capsule had slowed down sufficiently in the atmosphere, three parachutes were deployed which then gently brought it down into the ocean, where it was retrieved by a helicopter and deposited safely on the deck of an aircraft carrier that waited in the immediate vicinity.

The first successful mission for landing astronauts on the Moon commenced on July 16th, 1969. The massive Saturn V booster took off from The Kennedy Space Centre, Florida, with three astronauts on board—Neil Armstrong, Buzz Aldrin, and Michael Collins, blasting off from its launch pad in a fountain of flame and smoke. It took the craft three days to reach the Moon, and whilst in orbit around it, the Lunar Module, nicknamed Eagle, separated from the rest of the craft, and leaving Collins on board, Armstrong and Aldrin in the Lander descended to the Sea of Tranquility on the surface of the Moon on July 20th. The famous words 'The Eagle has landed' announced the safe arrival of the first men on the Moon, and when Neil Armstrong stepped on the surface for the first time, he uttered the memorable words—'A small step for (a) man; one giant leap for mankind.' Words that will live forever in history.

Armstrong and Aldrin spent a total of about 21½ hours on the lunar surface before blasting off in the Lunar Module to re-join Collins, who was piloting the Command Module, and returning safely to Earth, just as President Kennedy had promised.

Of course, perhaps the most memorable Moon landing attempt was that of Apollo 13 (a fateful number) to reach the Moon. Disaster struck with the explosion of an oxygen tank on the Service Module. This crippled the spacecraft, and the crew—James Lovell, Jack Swigert, and Fred Haise—had to abandon the mission and return to Earth. They suffered great hardship for the rest of the journey due to limited electric power, cabin heat, and oxygen supplies. It was only by the ingenuity and support of NASA ground staff and the cool-headed competence of the crew that disaster was avoided, and the space capsule returned safely to Earth on April 17th, and the astronauts given a heroes' welcome. These entire events were depicted in the epic Film Apollo 13, which starred Tom Hanks.

Several trips to the Moon followed between 1969 and 1972, totalling six in all, and ending with Apollo 17 in December 1972. Since then, no further manned space journeys to the Moon, or for that matter anywhere else in space, have been attempted. A certain public apathy towards manned space travel had developed, and now that the Russians had given up any hope of sending their cosmonauts to the Moon, the 'race to the Moon' ceased. After all, the Americans felt that their objectives had been met, and there seemed no further point in spending vast amounts of money in pursuing further Moon expeditions. This seems a great pity, because now almost half a century has passed and we are no further towards establishing a Moon Base on our nearest neighbour and using it as a stepping-stone for further space travel.

However, space exploration has continued by sending our unmanned spacecraft into the vicinity of every planet in the Solar System—Mercury, Venus, Mars, Jupiter, Saturn, Uranus, and Neptune, so our knowledge of not only our planets, but also most of their moons, has improved a hundredfold. I will deal with them briefly here:

Mercury is the planet nearest our Sun. It is very much like the Moon to look at. It spins on its axis very slowly—so slowly, that one side is roasting in the heat of the Sun whilst the other side freezes. It is the smallest planet in the Solar System and the least explored. The Mariner 10 (1975) and Messenger (2011) missions have been the only ones that have made close observations of the planet. It was named after the Greek god, Mercury, as it travels round the Sun so very quickly.

Venus is the 2nd planet nearest the Sun. It is the brightest planet in the night sky and was named after the Roman goddess of beauty. However, far from being beautiful, it is the most hellish planet in the Solar System, completely shrouded in cloud, with an atmosphere of mostly noxious, unbreathable carbon dioxide, which causes the planet to heat up in a 'greenhouse' effect, so the surface temperature is around 475°C, which is twice as hot as your domestic oven at its hottest. The Russians landed their craft, Venera 4, on the planet's surface in 1967, and it took a few pictures before it was frazzled out of existence by the intense heat. The American Mariner 2 spacecraft flew past Venus in 1962, and since then the Magellan spacecraft has been able to map the surface of the planet with its cloud-piercing radar. It showed a surface similar to Earth's with mountains and valleys, but no oceans, lakes, or rivers.

Mars, the 4th planet, is the most observed and explored of all the planets of the Solar System, besides Earth of course! It is deep red in appearance and is named after the Roman god of War. Observations of this planet go as far back as Copernicus in the 15th century. We have landed several robotic spacecraft on the planet's surface—the first two being Viking 1 and Viking 2 in 1976. They showed a red, barren, rocky desert, with mountains and a pink sky. It has a thin atmosphere of carbon dioxide and where there are clouds, these are of dust, as there is no water on the surface of the planet to form clouds of water-vapour. It is a cold, airless place and has no signs of life whatever. In 1997 the Pathfinder spacecraft bounce-landed on the surface of the planet, and a small robotic vehicle was released from it to explore surrounding rocks. In 2004, two robotic rovers, Spirit and Opportunity, landed on the surface and began their explorations, and then in 2012, another robotic rover, Curiosity, designed to carry out biological, climatic, and geological investigations, landed on the surface and at the time of writing is still going strong, sending back pictures as it roams around its neighbourhood. Mars is the only planet that we could consider sending manned spaceships to, although the logistics of sending men to survive in its inhospitable environment would be something of a challenge. However, it is feasible, and perhaps within this century it may just be possible to send humans to explore this planet. Mars has two moons, although they are nothing like ours, and are small, irregular potato-shaped objects, more akin to asteroids than true moons.

Jupiter is the 5th planet in the Solar System and is by far the largest. It is one of the so-called outer planets, and unlike the inner planets, does not have a rocky, solid surface, but is an enormous gas giant. It has several moons, the largest of which are Callisto, Ganymede, Europa, and Io. All these moons have solid surfaces, unlike their mother planet, and fly-bys of our spacecraft, such as Pioneer and Voyager, have taken very clear and detailed pictures of their surfaces, which are all very different from each other and of great interest—perhaps more so than their mother planet, as there is a possibility of future landings on their surfaces for exploring them further. In 1996, a space probe was actually sent into Jupiter's atmosphere of dense, marbled clouds, and a parachute was deployed as it sank through. The probe sent back signals of Jupiter's atmosphere, until it was crushed out of existence by the enormous pressures it encountered.

Saturn, the 6th planet from the Sun, is the most beautiful of all the planets. It is second in size only to Jupiter and is surrounded by a spectacular ring of icy particles that swirl around the golden planet. Again, it is a gas giant but, unlike Jupiter's marbled clouds, shows a rather bland uniform surface. Again, the Pioneer and Voyager spacecraft took spectacular photographs of the planet and of the rings. Like Jupiter, Saturn has several moons, the largest of which is Titan, which is an interesting moon as it has a substantial smoggy atmosphere. This proved so interesting, that the Cassini spacecraft was sent on a seven-year journey to Saturn, and soft-landed the Huygens probe on the surface of Titan. As it descended by parachute, it took photographs of the surface of this moon, which showed very earth-like features, like lakes of liquid methane and coastlines of land. Besides Titan, Saturn's other moons were photographed by the Pioneer and Voyager fly-bys, so we had a closer look at them than ever before.

Uranus is the 7th planet from the Sun, and is smaller than Saturn, but still one of the gas giants. It is tilted at such a peculiar angle that each of its poles in turn is pointing head-on towards the Sun. Voyager 2 flew by Uranus in 1986, and it was the first time we had a close look at the planet, because the best photographs from even the most powerful Earth-bound telescopes showed it only as a blurry blob, as it is so far away. Voyager 2 also took photographs of the moons of Uranus, seeing them clearly for the first time, and the surface features of some of them, like Miranda, intrigued scientists with their bizarre and geologically interesting features.

Neptune is the 8th and last planet in the Solar System. It, too, is a gas giant similar in size to Uranus. Pictures taken by the Voyager 2 spacecraft on its fly-by in 1989 revealed a pretty blue planet with white clouds scudding across its surface, indicating a very active weather system. Previously, scientists thought Neptune was too far away from the Sun to have enough heat to provide any weather system at all. In its fly-by, Voyager 2 also took photographs of one of Neptune's moons, Triton, and scientists were amazed that active geyser-like eruptions were spewing out nitrogen gas and dust several miles into space.

So with the various spacecraft that have explored the Solar System, we have at last seen close images of all the planets from Mercury to Neptune, and have unveiled some of their mysteries. The Pioneer and Voyager spacecraft continue on their journeys through outer space, and in their 37 years of travelling are the most distant man-made objects in outer space, and are still capable of sending and receiving signals from Earth. Voyager 1 is now leaving the influence of the Solar System (the heliopause) and is hurtling into deep space. It is the furthest man-made object ever to have travelled so far. It will reach the Oort cloud, a shell of comets lying about one light-year from the Sun, in about 20,000 years, and once it exits this, it will truly be in interstellar space. In many hundreds of thousands of years' time, it may eventually reach the vicinity of a neighbouring star, be captured by its gravity, and burn up if it ventured too close. Like its sister spacecraft Voyager 2, it is carrying a golden disc which contains scenes, greetings, music, and sounds from Earth, and should it ever be discovered by an alien civilization, it will tell them about our existence.

Going back to man in space, with the introduction of the Space Shuttle Program in 1972, as many as seven astronauts could be sent into Earth orbit with an ease undreamt of less than a decade earlier. The Space Shuttle was a re-usable spacecraft and resembled an aircraft in appearance. It had an enormous cargo bay that could carry such massive objects as the Hubble Space Telescope. It could also glide back into the Earth's atmosphere, and land on an airfield on Earth much like a plane, which obviated the hazardous and awkward process of landing astronauts by parachute into the ocean in their space capsule. A total of five Shuttles were built—Enterprise, Atlantis, Endeavour, Challenger, and Columbia.

However, disaster struck on the launch of Challenger on 28th January 1986. After lifting off from its launch pad on an extremely cold morning, a leak in the O-ring seal of one of the solid booster rockets caused a hot plume of gas to escape and burn through one of the struts holding the rocket to the external fuel tank and puncture it. Thus, a huge explosion followed when the fuel ignited, and the spacecraft completely disintegrated, with the loss of the entire crew.

Then again, on 1st February 2003, the Columbia Space Shuttle was lost sixteen minutes before it was expected to land on its return journey from space orbit. The cause was due to a piece of polystyrene foam hitting and damaging one of the leading edges of the Shuttle's wing during lift-off. This caused the heat encountered on re-entry to infiltrate the wing and damage the structure, resulting in complete disintegration of the Shuttle and killing all seven crew on board.

However, 135 successful missions were accomplished by the Space Shuttle during the 30 years of its operation, between 1981 and 2011, when the project was closed down. The last Shuttle flight was of the Atlantis in July 2011.

With the construction of the International Space Station in orbit around the Earth, it is necessary to replace the Space Shuttle with something similar, and the Commercial Crew Development program was initiated in 2010 for the purpose of creating commercially operated manned spacecraft, capable of delivering at least four crew members to the ISS and returning them back to Earth. It is expected that these spacecraft will become operational by around 2017.

Wars and Conflicts

Throughout history, we human beings have been in constant conflict with each other. Beginning at the very beginning, according to the Bible, the first recorded killing of one human being by another is from the Old Testament, when Cain slew his brother Abel. Since then, Man has been killing his neighbours by the hundreds, thousands, and even millions. We seem to be the only creatures that have this natural instinct for killing our own species, except perhaps for social insects, like ants, bees, and wasps, which often attack the hives or nests of other colonies of such insects, in a killing spree. But generally speaking, it is we humans that war with each other and kill on a massive scale.

I have listed below a few of the more warlike people on this planet, and a brief summary of their engagement in wars and conflicts.

The Egyptians

There are few written accounts by the ancient Egyptians of warfare between themselves and any hostile neighbours to the north, mainly people like the Hittites. The only evidence of such conflicts is depictions of battle scenes on temple walls. Some of them show the triumphant and victorious warrior Pharaoh, Rameses II, slaying his enemy Hittites at the Battle of Kadesh in 1274 B.C. However, the ancient Egyptians were fortunately placed geographically from attack by hostile neighbours, and were a united people both culturally and ethnically. They prospered, and their cities did not usually require defensive walls to keep the people secure. Nevertheless, they did develop weapons and war machines like their chariots, which were of an efficient and sophisticated design and which they used to great effect in their battles.

The Greeks

In ancient Greek history, one of the earliest and most detailed accounts of warfare was in Homer's Iliad and Odyssey, written in the 12th or 13th century B.C., when the Greeks besieged the city of Troy after Paris abducted the beautiful Helen, wife of Menelaus, king of Sparta. The ensuing war lasted for ten years, and finally, when the Greek army was unable to breach the walls of the city, they pretended to withdraw, and left behind them a large wooden horse, which concealed a raiding party inside. The Trojans, thinking this had been a gift left behind by the Greeks, took the horse through the city gates. While they celebrated their supposed victory and had drunk themselves into a stupor, the troops inside the horse silently emerged and opened the city gates to let in the rest of the Greek army, who soon overwhelmed the city, massacring the male citizens and carrying off the women in victorious triumph. The old saying, 'beware of the Greeks bearing gifts,' originates from this incident, and it simply means not to trust your enemies.

The Greeks were a warlike people, particularly under the leadership of Alexander the Great in 336 B.C., and they invaded many of their surrounding countries, like Persia—

when they overthrew the Persian King Darius III, and conquered the entire Persian Empire. Alexander's invasions continued into India in 326 B.C., but the campaign lasted so long that his troops became war-weary, homesick, and discontented, so he was forced to abandon his efforts to conquer the country, and return home. He also invaded and occupied Egypt, and he founded the city of Alexandria, which still bears his name to this day. The Greek invaders, however, were welcomed by the Egyptian people as they were under occupation by the Persians, and Alexander was heralded as a liberator, given godly status, and pronounced 'Master of the Universe'. Even their coins depicted him adorned with ram's horns—a symbol of his divinity. The Greek invaders adopted much of the Egyptian culture and even its religion when they set up their Ptolemaic Kingdom, and the much-famed queen, Cleopatra, was of Greek and not Egyptian descent as popularly supposed.

The Spartans

The Spartans were a very warlike people and even young boys were taken away from their mothers and trained in military combat from a young age. The very term 'Spartan' means someone who is unsparing and uncompromising in discipline and judgment. The reputation of Sparta as a courageous, land-fighting force was unequalled. There have been many epic films made about their battles, such as a small force of Spartan soldiers making a legendary last stand at the

Battle of Thermopylae against the massive Persian army, inflicting heavy casualties on the Persian forces before being finally encircled and put to the sword. They also had wars with the Athenians and defeated them in the Peloponnesian War between 431 and 404 B.C.

The Romans

One of the most successful imperial and military powers in history was ancient Rome. Roman society was governed by a strong military ethos, which led to incessant warfare, conquest, and the expansion of the Roman Empire, which encircled the whole of the Mediterranean area, and extended as far as Britain. They conquered, dominated, and ruled the countries that they occupied. But at the same time, they brought with them their culture, language, and civilization. Their soldiers were so well disciplined and trained that few enemies could stand up to them. They were also well armed and extremely courageous. Their armies marched across most of Europe, and where they occupied, they set up a well-administrated and organised system of government. Unlike the Greeks, who excluded foreigners and subjected peoples from political participation, the Romans incorporated conquered peoples into its social and political system, and allies and subjects who adopted Roman ways and customs were often made Roman citizens. They were quite ruthless in warfare and gave no quarter to the enemy, which is why they were so feared by their opponents. They were also very tenacious in the pursuit of their enemies, and when a gladiator, Spartacus, rebelled and raised an army that fought against their Roman masters, causing them a great deal of trouble and some military defeats, Pompey led the Romans and pursued him endlessly, finally trapping him and his rebels with their backs to the sea, and defeated them. This story of Spartacus has also been made into epic Hollywood films, television series, and documentaries.

The Roman Empire lasted over one millennia, and was one of the most dominant in western history.

The Vikings

These fierce Scandinavian seafaring warriors crossed the seas in their longboats and raided and colonised wide areas of Europe from the 9th to the 11th century. Britain became a target for these pagan Danish, Norwegian, and Swedish invaders, and they conquered and occupied the ancient kingdoms of East Anglia and Northumbria and Mercia in the 8th century. Despite being unable to subdue the Saxon king, Alfred the Great in Wessex, much of England was in Danish hands and ultimately the country became part of the empire under the Viking king, Canute, who became king of England from 1016 to 1035. The invasions of these Scandinavian warriors had a great influence on English culture, social structure, and place and personal names, which exist to this day.

The Mongols

Under the leadership of Genghis Khan, this warlord and military genius brought together the various nomadic tribes of the Mongolian people as a fighting force that swept across the steppes on horseback, raiding, destroying, and plundering wherever they went. These savage hordes eventually conquered most of Asia and their empire ultimately stretched from the Adriatic Sea to the Pacific coast of China, making it the largest land empire in history. They were merciless to their enemies, which gained them a reputation for savagery and terror. The Mongol Empire, which began in 1206, lasted until 1368 under Genghis Khan and his successors.

The Ottomans

By wars of conquest, the Ottoman Empire (created by Turkish tribes in Anatolia) became one of the most powerful empires in the world during the 15th and 16th centuries and lasted for more than 600 years. In the reign of Suleiman the Magnificent, it stretched across most of southeast Europe, Western Asia, the Caucasus, North Africa, and the Horn of Africa. Its capital was the city of Constantinople, which had previously been the capital city of the Christian Byzantine Empire, which they conquered. As their empire spread, so did their religion of Islam, but they did not force the peoples of the countries they occupied to convert. Their army was once amongst the most advanced fighting forces in the world, being one of the first to use muskets and cannons. However, like all empires, the Ottoman Empire finally fell and was dissolved in the aftermath of the First World War. Then new political regimes emerged and spread as far as Algeria to the west. These included Turkey, several Balkans nations, and all the Middle-Eastern states, such as modern-day Iran, Iraq, and Syria.

The British

Throughout their history, the English had always been engaged in warfare—both internally with the Scots and externally, particularly with the French and Spanish. Being protected by a narrow strip of water, the English Channel, England was largely protected from invasion, except the Norman Conquest of 1066 by William the Conqueror who defeated the Saxon King, Harold II, at the Battle of Hastings, whereupon the earlier Saxon kings were replaced by Norman ones.

Britain also played a major role in religious wars like the Crusades between 1095 and 1291 where the Knight Templars invaded Jerusalem and took control of the ancient city. Even kings, like the famed Richard the Lionheart of England, took part in the Crusades, and battled with their Muslim opponents led by Saladin.

Internal conflicts usually took place in a struggle for political power between kings, such as The Wars of the Roses (1455-85) between the house of Lancaster (represented by a red rose), and the house of York (represented by a white rose), which resulted in victory by Henry VII of Lancaster over Richard III of York at Bosworth on August 22nd, 1485. However, the two houses were merged into one by the marriage of Henry VII, who was better known as Henry Tudor, to Elizabeth of York, the daughter of Edward IV. So the two roses—red and white— were merged into one, which became the Tudor Rose, and the emblem of the Tudor dynasty.

Another struggle for internal power within the country was the English Civil War, which began in 1642 between the Parliamentarians (Roundheads) led by Oliver Cromwell, and the Royalists who were loyal to the King, Charles I of England. This war also took its toll of human lives and divided the country. The reason for the conflict was largely because Charles was an autocratic ruler who would not relinquish any of his power or authority to the English Parliament. Eventually the war led to his downfall and the victorious Roundheads executed him in 1649, whereupon Britain was declared a Commonwealth with Cromwell as Lord Protector.

However, after Cromwell's death in 1658, the republican experiment faltered, and although he was succeeded by his son Richard, the people had become weary of living under Cromwell's puritanical rule. So the late king's son, Charles, who had taken refuge in France for the duration of the war, was invited back to the country where he was restored to the throne of England as Charles II in 1660.

Although English soil has soaked up much blood on its battlefields, being a seafaring nation many of its battles were also fought at sea. For example, when the Spanish threatened to invade England by sending a fleet of 130 ships and overthrow Queen Elizabeth I of England, the British fleet under the command of Sir Francis Drake, albeit with the help of stormy seas, defeated the Armada in the English Channel in 1588.

Another significant naval battle was in 1805 during the Napoleonic Wars, when the British fleet, headed by Admiral Lord Nelson aboard HMS Victory, defeated thirty-three French and Spanish ships off the coast of Spain. However, the heroic Lord Nelson was fatally wounded in this encounter and a memorial is dedicated to him at Trafalgar Square in the city of London.

Then, during World War II, a very famous sea battle took place on 24th May 1941 when, in an attempt to stop the German battleship Bismarck from entering the Atlantic, two British warships, HMS Prince of Wales and HMS Hood took on the superior German vessel and, as a consequence, HMS Hood was destroyed when a shell hit her ammunition magazine, and she exploded and sank with the loss of all but three of her crew.

It would be impossible to recount all the wars, battles, and conflicts in which the peoples of the British Isles have been engaged. But among the most significant are: The Crusades (1096 –1291); The Hundred Years' War (1337-1453); English Civil War (1642-51); Jacobite Rebellion (1715 & 1745); American War of Independence (1775-83); Napoleonic Wars

(1803-15); Crimean War (1853-56); Boer War (1880-81 & 1899-1902); Indian Mutiny (1857-58). And, of course, the two greatest wars in history—World War I (1914-18) and World War II (1939-45) with Germany and its Axis powers.

The French

Like the British, the French were engaged in wars for most of their history. Their main enemy was the English, and many battles were fought on the Continent and in British colonies like India and North America, in a struggle for supremacy, where the British invariably emerged victorious. The most significant conflict in their history was when the French people rose against their king, Louis XVI of France in the French Revolution in 1789 with the storming of the Bastille. This resulted in the execution of their king by guillotine, and also his wife, Marie Antoinette, and France became a Republic.

This did not last long, for in the early part of the 19th century, a French military and political leader, Napoleon Bonaparte, rose to power and was crowned Emperor of France in 1804. He started a campaign to gain control of most of continental Europe in the Napoleonic Wars and build an empire. However, his campaign came to grief when he attempted to invade Russia in 1812. Due to Russia's 'scorched earth' tactics, which was the destruction of all crops, food, and other resources in advance of the invading French army, this together with the harshness of the Russian winter, soon forced the French to retreat, bringing an end to Napoleon's invasion.

The Napoleonic Wars eventually came to an end in 1815 when the French forces were defeated in the Battle of Waterloo by the Duke of Wellington and his army, and Napoleon was eventually captured and imprisoned on the island of St. Helena where he died in 1821. His remains are held in a tomb at Les Invalides in Paris, France.

Besides the Napoleonic Wars, France was deeply implicated in both World Wars—the largest wars in human history, and which involved nations rather than just countries. In the First World War (1914-18), under the leadership of Kaiser Wilhelm II Emperor of Germany, the bulk of the fighting in Europe occurred in Belgium, Luxembourg, France, and along what came to be known as the Western Front. It mainly took the form of trench warfare, where opposing forces occupied trenches with little advancement or gain in territory. The war ended in November 1918 with an Armistice being signed between England and France and the defeated Germany.

In the Second World War (1939-45), France fell to the German invading forces under the dictatorship of Adolph Hitler, despite the defensive barricade built by the French, the Maginot Line, which they outflanked. The German army pushed deep into France and eventually, undefended Paris fell to the invading army on 14th June 1940. The country remained under German occupation until the liberation by allied forces, commencing with the D-Day invasion on 6th of June 1944 on the beaches of Normandy. Germany was finally defeated in May 1945 with the surrender of German forces.

The Americans

The first war in North America was the War of Independence fought by the colonial inhabitants of the country to gain freedom from their British masters. It began in 1775 during the reign of George III King of England. With the help of France, the colonialists were eventually successful in defeating the English forces, and on 19th October 1781, Lord Cornwallis of the British forces capitulated to General George Washington, who became the first President of America. The war was over and the American colonies had won their independence.

Except for skirmishes and conflicts with the natives of the continent, the Red Indians, as also the Mexicans over the annexation of Texas in the battle for the Alamo, no major wars were fought on the continent, unlike those in Europe.

However, the cruellest war of all was the American Civil War, which began in 1861 and continued to 1865. This war was between the Northern and Southern States of America, and had its origins in the fractious issue of slavery. The Southern States of America had been importing black slave labour from Africa to run the prosperous plantations in the South, and when Abraham Lincoln became President of the country, he opposed the expansion of slavery into other United States' territories, and wanted the emancipation of all slaves. This led to seven Southern slave states declaring their secession from the rest of the country, and they formed the Confederate

States of America. Bloody combat followed, with General Ulysses S. Grant leading the Yankees (the Northerners), and General Robert E. Lee commanding the Confederates (Southerners). It put family against family and neighbour against neighbour in bloody conflict, which resulted in an enormous loss of life on both sides. Fortunately, foreign powers like Britain and France did not intervene or take sides in the conflict, so it was largely an internal issue. A decisive battle took place between the two sides at Gettysburg in 1863, and in the ensuing years, the Southern forces capitulated.

Of course, the now United States of America played a major role in both World Wars, and their immense military strength and resources tipped the scales in favour of the allies. With the attack on the American naval base at Pearl Harbour in the Hawaiian Islands by the Japanese on 7th December 1941, war with Japan was declared. The Americans took on the brunt of the invasion by Japan to expand its empire into the Pacific, and many battles ensued with the regaining of captured territories, like the Solomon Islands, the Marshall Islands, Guadalcanal, the Philippines, and the Marianas. Eventually, it attacked the mainland of Japan with the detonation of two atomic bombs at Hiroshima and Nagasaki, in August 1945, which brought an end to the war with Japan but caused the death of over 150,000 civilian Japanese and utterly destroyed both cities. In May of the same year, the Americans—along with their British and Russian allies—also defeated Germany.

Since the end of the last World War, America—now the supreme world power—has been involved in at least five major conflicts. The first of these was against the spread of Communism in South-East Asia, when the Americans with the help of their allies, entered into a war with North Korea in 1950 to prevent South Korea being invaded by its hostile neighbour. This conflict is still unsettled, though the two sides, the North and South Koreans, are in a state of a cease-fire, divided by a strip of land called the Demilitarised Zone.

The second was the Vietnam War in 1959 when the Americans did the same thing to assist the South Vietnamese against Communism from its neighbour, North Vietnam. The Vietnam War ended in complete disaster for the Americans, who had to pull out in a rapid debacle. The war was unpopular in America and did not have the support of most of the population because they felt American soldiers were being killed by the thousands in a useless war.

Then in the 1990s, war with Iraq commenced when the Americans bombed the Iraqi invaders out of existence to force their withdrawal from Kuwait, which they had occupied under the directions of Iraqi leader, Saddam Hussain. A cease-fire with Iraq followed, with a no-fly zone being imposed on Iraq.

The war with the Iraqis re-commenced in 2003 when the West felt threatened by Saddam Hussain, whom they thought was making weapons of mass destruction to use against the West. The country was invaded again and occupied by American and British forces, and Saddam overthrown, eventually captured, and then executed by the new Iraqi government. This took place after the attack on the Twin Towers in New York City by Al Qaeda terrorists, and was part of the American war against terrorism.

In continuation of their war against terror, Afghanistan was also invaded in 2001 and occupied by the Americans and their allies, mainly the British, to eradicate the Taliban, who had been in control of the country, and who had links to Al Qaeda. Their leader, Osama bin Laden—who was the culprit responsible for the terrorist movement, went into hiding but was eventually discovered and killed in Pakistan in 2013 by an American covert operation. The war in Afghanistan still continues at the time of writing; although there are plans for complete US troop withdrawals by the end of 2016.

The Russians

Historically, Russia always felt isolated from the rest of Western Europe. It has had many wars throughout its history starting from 1480, in battles with the Golden Horde to free themselves from Mongol rule. They engaged in other wars with neighbouring people like the Poles, Lithuanians, Swedes, and the Ottoman Turks, as also wars with the Japanese on their Eastern frontier. Their main allies were the Ukrainian Cossacks, who were a warrior-like people and did their fighting mostly on horseback. Russia had such prominent leaders as Peter the Great who proclaimed Russia and empire, and Ivan the Terrible who became the first Tsar of Russia.

Past invasions of Russia usually came to grief due to the vastness of the country and the terrible winter weather. Napoleon failed in his attempts to conquer Russia and so did Hitler during the Second World War, when his troops became bogged down on the outskirts of Moscow and were unable to be adequately supplied with ammunition and provisions. However, Russia suffered terrible casualties in World War II with the figures of civilian and military dead numbering almost 20 million, whereas the allies suffered only a fraction of that number.

Before the end of the First World War, the Russian people rebelled against their Tsar, Nicholas II, and so began the Russian Revolution. In the Civil War that ensued, the Tsar and his entire family were placed under house-arrest and after being denied sanctuary in England by Nicholas's cousin King George V of England, were eventually murdered by the revolutionaries; a very sad chapter in history. In the conflict between the anti-Communist White Russians and the new Soviet regime with its Red Army, the Bolshevik Communists triumphed, and under the leadership of Vladimir Lenin, gained control of the country which then became the first Communist power, under a new name—the Union of the Soviet Socialist Republic, or USSR for short. The civil war, however, heavily damaged the Russian economy and infrastructure, and the famine that ensued claimed up to 5 million victims.

Following Lenin's death in 1921, and under the new leadership of Joseph Stalin, the Russians allied themselves to

Britain and America during World War II and eventually drove the German invaders back beyond their borders and into Germany itself, where they laid siege to Berlin and finally took the city.

What ensued after the end of the War was what became known as the Cold War, where Russia drew an 'iron curtain' between itself and the West, and became hostile towards its former allies. They refused to relinquish control of the countries they had liberated in the war, such as Poland, Czechoslovakia, and Hungary, as also the city of Berlin, which had to be divided into zones between the allies and themselves. They even went to the lengths of erecting a wall dividing the city, which became known as the Berlin Wall, to keep the people living in East Berlin sealed in. They also began an arms race with America and developed the H-bomb by covertly stealing secrets from the USA. However, a sort-of-peace prevailed under the threat of mass extinction should one country attack the other with nuclear weapons.

This Cold War continued until 1991 when the Soviet regime was overthrown and a democratic government installed in its place. However, the Russians still treat the West with suspicion and though relinquishing its formerly occupied territories, relationships between Russia and the West are still strained.

The Japanese
The military history of Japan is characterised by long periods of feudal wars between various tribes existing on the

Japanese Archipelago. Japan was always a war-like nation, with their Samurai warriors who fought on horseback clad in suits of armour, and who followed a strict code of honour in their battles. Outside threats, such as invasion by the Mongols in the 13th century, were successfully repulsed. They also had wars with Korea and China and were engaged in conflict with Russia during the Russo-Japanese War in 1904-05, and were the first Asian nation to successfully win a war against a European power.

From the 16th century, the Japanese felt threatened by Western powers, like the Americans, particularly when they established a naval base at Pearl Harbour in the Hawaiian Islands. Japan's ambitions of expanding their empire into South-East Asia and the Pacific were frustrated by the American presence in the Pacific, so on 7th December 1941, they attacked Pearl Harbour by aircraft sent from the aircraft carriers of the Imperial Japanese Navy that lay in range of the Hawaiian Islands.

The attack came as a complete surprise to the Americans and considerable damage was done to the naval base, including the sinking and damaging of as many as 18 warships of the Pacific fleet anchored there, including four battleships, and several cruisers and destroyers. Many American aircraft were also destroyed on the ground, and heavy loss of life was inflicted on the people stationed at the base—both civilian and military. Not surprisingly, war was declared by the United States the following day with President Franklin D. Roosevelt's famous words to proclaim the 7th of December 1941 as, 'A date which will live in infamy.'

Fortunately, all three of the American aircraft carriers, Enterprise, Lexington, and Saratoga, were at sea when the attack on Pearl Harbour took place, so in the later stages of the war with Japan that ensued, the Americans had these ships which were vital in the campaigns to regain control of the various islands in the Pacific that the Japanese formerly invaded and captured.

The war with Japan, which formed part of the Second World War as Japan had allied itself to Germany, went on for four long years with considerable loss of life, particularly the Japanese, and culminated with the dropping of A-bombs on Hiroshima and Nagasaki in August 1945, which brought an end to the war. Since then, Japan has lived in peace with the disbandment of its army and all military ambitions and concentrated more on commercial enterprise.

The Germans

Formerly part of Prussia, the German nation came into being in 1871 by the bringing together of dozens of German-speaking kingdoms, by Prussian Prime Minister Otto von Bismarck to form the German Empire, the so-called Second Reich. The empire acquired colonies in Africa, Asia, and the Pacific, and although the peoples of the areas it was formed of were not directly involved in conflicts as a nation, they were often referred to by the ancient Romans as Germanic tribes.

It was not until the advent of the First World War, under the German Emperor Kaiser Wilhelm II, that Germany and its allies (mainly Austria, Hungary, and Turkey) became involved in war with Great Britain and its allies (mainly France, Russia, Italy, Japan, and later the USA) in a major conflict. The root cause of the war was the assassination of Archduke Ferdinand of Austria by Serbian nationalists whilst he was on a visit to Sarajevo in Bosnia. This led Germany to ally itself with Austria and attack Serbia whilst Britain, France, and Russia formed an allegiance to oppose this threat.

From such small beginnings, this escalated into a major conflict and, as a result, millions died on the battlefields of Europe and elsewhere. It was mainly an Imperial war between emperors like Kaiser Wilhelm of Germany, the Tsar of Russia Nicholas II, and George V King of England, who were all first cousins! The war was finally concluded in 1918 with the defeat of Germany and the signing of the Armistice, but it took its toll on human lives with the slaughter, carnage, and destruction it caused. Germany's economy was also decimated in its aftermath, when a single loaf of bread cost 200 billion marks. The war also resulted in the Bolshevik Revolution in Russia and the destabilisation of Europe, which laid the groundwork of World War II.

The Second World War (1939-45) was the bloodiest conflict in history, claiming about 50 million lives, mostly in Russia and China. The root cause was the rise to power in Germany of dictator Adolph Hitler and his quest to establish the Third Reich for Germany. The war started with his invasion of Poland in August 1939 when Great Britain and France declared war on Germany, although they had tried to negotiate a peace accord prior to that. The German armies then commenced a blitzkrieg (lightning warfare) sweeping across the whole of Europe, and France fell to the Germans, as did most of the remaining countries, except Switzerland who remained neutral.

Britain and its allies fought a brave and determined struggle against the might of the German war machine, but it was mainly the English Channel that saved them from invasion, and Hitler's decision to attack Russia, which was his greatest mistake. Later, in 1941, after the attack on Pearl Harbour by the Japanese, who allied themselves to the Germans, the United States entered the war, and with their help, Britain was able to survive and was eventually led to victory with the defeat of Germany in 1945, the same year as victory in Japan.

The Israelis

The Israelis, or as they were known in ancient times—the Israelites—were in constant conflict with their neighbours throughout their early history. The first recorded battle, according to Biblical texts, was the battle of Jericho, when the follower of Moses, the Prophet Joshua, laid siege to the city which resulted, with the help of God, 'in the walls of the city to come tumbling down'. When they entered the Promised Land, they were in constant conflict with their neighbours like the Philistines, Assyrians, and Babylonians.

However, being driven out of their lands over 2,000 years ago, the Jewish people have lived, sometimes as unwelcome guests, in foreign homelands, and except for persecution by the people of their host countries, particularly the Nazis of Germany during the Holocaust, they lived their lives in comparative peace and did not involve themselves much in the politics of the countries in which they resided, but instead concentrated mainly on commerce and finance, until that is, they became a Jewish State in 1948.

This happened as a consequence of World War II when, after suffering at the hands of their German persecutors which resulted in the extermination of almost all the Jewish population in Europe, they decided that they should return to the country God had promised them—the land of Zion, and that land was Palestine, now occupied by Arab people and under British administration. They immigrated in droves to Palestine in a mass exodus, and despite attempts by the British authorities to curb their numbers, they entered the country nevertheless and established themselves there. The West felt some sympathy towards them, and under the auspices of the United Nations, Palestine was divided up in 1948 to give the Jewish people a separate state and a homeland, much to the consternation and fury of their Arab neighbours. From then on, conflict with the neighbouring Arabs was assured.

There have been at least three major conflicts between Israel and its Arab neighbours, commencing with a threatened invasion in 1948 when the armies of Egypt, Lebanon, Syria,

Jordan, and Iraq mustered on the borders of Israel. The Israeli army repulsed the attack and acquired control of further territories beyond those originally allocated to them by the United Nations.

The second of these conflicts took place in 1967 in what popularly became known as the Six Day War, when Israel was again threatened by invasion by its hostile neighbours. Israel attacked and destroyed the Egyptian air bases on the ground, thus gaining superiority of the skies. They also gained control of the Golan Heights from Syria, the Gaza Strip, and Sinai Peninsula from Egypt and the West Bank, including East Jerusalem from Jordan.

The third major conflict was in 1973 popularly known as the Yom Kippur War as it began on the holiest day in Judaism. Egyptian and Syrian forces crossed ceasefire lines to enter the Sinai Peninsula and Golan Heights, which had previously been captured by Israel in the former conflict of 1967. It took Israel by surprise, but when they had recovered, they counter-attacked and managed to repulse the invading forces.

A stalemate ensued in the subsequent years, but eventually Israel relinquished Sinai after peace negotiations with Egypt in 1979. However, Israel still continues to hold on to Jerusalem, which is a major sticking point and continues to this day. Meanwhile, millions of Palestinian refugees have been deprived of their homeland and live in exile in refugee camps in Lebanon, Syria, and Jordan. This situation gave rise to the Palestinian Liberation Organisation, or PLO, who carried out campaigns of terror under its late leader Yasser Arafat from 1964 to 1993 when the PLO finally recognised the right of Israel to exist. The right to exist has always been an issue with the Israelis, because having suffered extermination in Europe at the hands of the Nazis, they now feel under constant threat by their Arab neighbours, some of whom refuse to accept this right.

Instability in the world at large persists to this day, particularly on the African continent where ethnic conflicts have resulted in genocide, such as that in Rwanda. Places like the Gold Coast and Somalia in the Horn of Africa are also trouble spots, and in North Africa, Muslim countries like Tunisia, Libya, and Egypt have overthrown their leaders in what is termed 'The Arab Spring'. The conflict has spread further into the Middle East with the Syrian Civil War raging in a struggle to overthrow the Ba'ath government under Syrian leader President Hafez al-Assad. More recently, the Islamic State fundamentalists are gradually gaining control of parts of Syria and Iraq, and their threat of terrorism is a worry to Western powers. Iran is also a belligerent country and despite its denials, is believed to be on the verge of producing a nuclear bomb. Meanwhile, Israel stands in the centre of it all, poised to attack should it feel threatened by any of its hostile neighbours.

All this conflict throughout human history has resulted in millions upon millions of deaths. But one has to ask oneself that since we have no natural predators, what would the human population numbers have been were it not for all these war casualties? Perhaps it is part of nature's way of controlling the numbers of our species?

Furthermore, it is an ironical fact that war has always spurred on advances in technology, and considerable progress has been made under these conditions. For example, our research into nuclear physics to produce the first atomic bomb might never have gotten underway were it not to produce such a superior weapon of war; or the development of rocket technology such as Germany's V2 weapon, which has enabled our ventures into outer space. War justifies the great financial costs involved in such projects, where money seems to be no object. It is a typical case of 'the end justifying the means'. The arms race has continued throughout history to gain superior weapons to those of the enemies, and were it not for this, we may very well have stagnated as far as technical progress is concerned.

The Human Experience

The human brain is probably the most complicated thing in the entire Universe. It is the receptacle for all our thoughts, ideas, beliefs, and memories. However, when we talk about the mind, it is rather different. The difference between the brain and the mind can be likened to your laptop computer. Whereas the computer represents the biological brain, the software and data you feed into it represents the stored information, which we can imagine as our thoughts, ideas, beliefs, and memories. Of course, a computer does not have a mind, as it has not the ability to think.

The ability to think is unique to us humans. After all, most animals, fish, and insects have a brain too, even an ant. However, it does not have the ability to think, and therefore has a brain but not a mind.

Creatures such as ants have a miniscule speck of brain matter compared to us humans. It gives the insect the ability to move its limbs and mandibles, to eat and be aware of its environment, thus making it conscious of its surroundings. It does not think, and goes about its business following a pattern of behaviour that seems to work very much like a computer program. An ant will always be an ant and behave like an ant. You won't see an ant behaving like a cockroach or visa-versa. All this information is carried through the generations by its genes.

In addition, they do not have a complicated nervous system like we have, which is why they do not seem to feel pain as we do and don't roll around in anguish should they lose a limb.

Nevertheless, they do have the instinct to eat and reproduce, build their nests, and gather their food. They also have the ability to defend themselves with their bites and stings, and also have a sense of danger when they feel threatened, although they have no concept of death. This self-preservation seems to be built into the fabric of every living creature. They can sense their environment through their primitive eyes and their antennae.

Compared to us humans, ants have super-human strength, and can carry objects several times their own bodyweight. In addition, an ant can drop to the ground from a height of several feet without being harmed, so in some ways they have physical properties that are far superior to ours. They can run faster, climb walls, and even fly, when the males of the colony develop wings. Termites, too, build structures that are far larger, in relation to their size, than some of our cities. Population-wise, they are doing rather better than we are as well, as it is estimated that there are about 50 quadrillion ants to our population of 7 billion, that is in the ratio of about 7 million plus ants to every human on Earth!

Biologically, we share many of our organs with other creatures on Earth—brains, stomachs, hearts, lungs, and livers, etc., but it is our minds that are so different. Although some animals, particularly elephants and our domestic pets, seem to have the ability to remember and recognise old friends and events, they do not seem to be as self-aware as we are. A cat, for example, does not seem to recognise its reflection in a mirror. Or, if it were to jump on top of a hot stove, it may have the instinct to learn never to jump on the stove again, but may not remember the event. However, animals, particularly our house pets, do seem to have emotions and moods rather similar to ours. They can show affection, fear, guilt, anger, and aggression. They also seem to have a personality, and can be either bad-tempered or good-natured. But, of course, they cannot conceive who or what we are, whereas even a two-year old infant can.

However, animals have certain senses that are far superior to ours—their acute hearing and sense of smell. They always seem to know where they are. For example, a bee will always find its way back to its hive. Fish, like salmon, will always return to the place of their spawning, even travelling the lengths of the oceans to return there to breed. Birds will migrate to certain locations during the winter and summer months. Finding their way about and navigating the Earth is something of a mystery. Scientists think they use the Earth's magnetic field as a navigation aid, like us with our GPS satellites. They also have the ability to fly, swim, leap, and burrow, and some creatures, like ducks, are endowed with the ability to waddle, swim, and fly. So their locomotion is far superior to us humans who can only walk. It is only with our inventiveness in creating machines to do this work for us that we can achieve these methods of travel. Before that, we used the superior speed and strength of animals, like horses, to do this work for us.

Our relationship with animals has always been a close one throughout our history. Not only have we used them to help us get about, but as one of our most important food sources— meat. We have gained their trust by domesticating cattle, sheep, pigs, and chickens to slaughter them without the need to hunt these difficult-to-catch creatures, thus ensuring a regular food supply. We consume about 218 million tons of meat per year. Not only do we consume meat, but also our advanced fishing techniques catch about 93 million tons of fish annually. Plant life is fully exploited by us humans too, and we have used wood as fuel, and building material for our houses, and some of our most important food sources are grain, fruit, and vegetables.

Our relationship with our pets is a very close one. Who doesn't love their dog or cat? Sometimes we love them and feel their loss more keenly than one of our closest human friends or relatives. The only reason for this is one of companionship. Long gone are the days when we kept a dog simply to aid us in hunting, or a cat to catch vermin. They are our faithful and loving companions. Even fish are kept in aquariums or glass bowls, but we rarely keep insects as pets.

However, one great advantage we have over our animal friends is by being bipeds, not having the need to use our arms and hands to aid us in walking, thus leaving these free to work for us. It is only having manipulative hands, which most other creatures lack, that gave our early ancestors the ability to make tools. This, working in conjunction with a large brain, made us who we are today—a highly intelligent and civilized species.

However, our brain has its limitations. Like a cup, you can only fill it until the liquid reaches the brim. We can only imagine to the limits of our own experience. For example, try imagining a bright colour other than the ones we see around us. We cannot do it because it is beyond the limits of our experience. Those born blind cannot see, therefore they have no conception of vision. Similarly, a deaf person cannot imagine sound, because it is outside his or her experience. He or she may know about these things, but they cannot comprehend them. However, fortunately, their other senses of touch, smell, and taste seem to become more acute in comprehending the world about them, and seem to make up somewhat for the loss of their other senses.

Communication between our species has helped tremendously in making us the advanced civilization that we have become. Both the spoken and written word has helped share information, so our brains have become extended beyond the realms of its immediate surroundings. Imagine a child stranded in the jungles or on a remote island without any information about the outside world. There have been cases of children apparently being brought up by wolves and such, who had no experience of the outside world, and have therefore been nearly impossible to educate. Shared experiences by communication have almost caused the brain to extend, and with the development of the Internet, modern civilization has almost become one super-brain.

In the past, many inventions and discoveries were kept secret, and perhaps only passed down to a close member of the next generation. This has been particularly prevalent in Eastern cultures, where the father's skill or knowledge was only passed down to his son, who then would possess these unique capabilities to ensure his future in life. However, in the Western world, all information was shared by the publication of books and written papers, even in repressive societies where these writings would be considered heretical— particularly scientific knowledge that disagreed with religious thought.

It is considered by some that the mind is not related to the physical body but is a separate conscious state. In other words, our thought processes cannot be described as something in the realms of physics.

What Makes Us Human?

What makes us human and so different to the animals around us? Most religious theologies consider that all humans have a soul that enables us to go to the hereafter following our physical death. It is only because we have this realisation of death, which other animals do not seem to share, that we have conceived of an afterlife—a life after death. This goes right back to the beginning of religious thought.

Almost all faiths promise an afterlife, and sometimes this is considered more important than our physical existence on Earth. The ancient Egyptian Pharaohs spent their life in preparation for their eventual death, having huge structures like the pyramids built. Religious monks spent their lives in prayer and meditation, hoping their souls would be saved in salvation and not sent down to suffer the tortures of Hell. Even today, religious fundamentalists, like suicide bombers, sacrifice their lives with the promise of Paradise, which they believe will be granted should they forsake their lives for a religious ideal. The instances go on and on.

The human soul is thought to be a spiritual rather than a physical thing. In other words, it is not the physical us—our looks and appearance, but the spiritual us, which is our inner-self—our personality and true identity.

The soul is thought to have certain qualities, for instance to know the difference between right and wrong. It possesses feelings such as love, truth, compassion, and faith. All these are thought to be godly qualities. Hate, vanity, greed, and cruelty are thought to be un-godly characteristics and are considered evil. These are the two faces of our humanity. Also, unlike animals that do not share our characteristics, we have a conscience that guides us through the path of right and wrong. You are supposed to act in accordance with your conscience.

Religious belief is thought to guide us along the path of righteousness, and has had a great influence on human society. All religions preach good behaviour against bad behaviour, which is why we are told to respect our fellow humans and not steal, murder, or commit adultery. These rules apply to ensure a harmonious and orderly society.

However, this is not always the case, and in times of war, no holds are barred, and an enemy is given no quarter should his beliefs and ideologies conflict with ours. In other words, the rules seem to apply more within our own society or culture rather than between societies and cultures outside our own. This is why wars are so commonplace between different nations throughout history, because they were different or thought differently, and were, therefore, considered the enemy. This has gone on from ancient times to the present day.

In antiquity, so-called civilized societies, like the Romans, behaved in a barbaric way, persecuting Christian converts to suffer horrific deaths in their arenas for purely entertainment purposes. As far as they were concerned, the more terrible the death, the more amusement it provided. They rejoiced in the pain, suffering, and terror of the poor unfortunates thrown to the lions.

Through the years, religious persecutions continued even by the Church, and the cruellest and most painful tortures were devised to coerce the victim to confess, or to renounce their religious views. These devices took the form of the rack, the thumbscrew, the iron maiden, and other horrific instruments of torture.

Public executions that took place in countries such as England were particularly gruesome, like being hung, drawn, and quartered. In this procedure, the victim was hung until he was almost dead, then his body taken down and placed on a bench where it was cut in pieces, starting with his genitals, and then he was disembowelled, and his entrails thrown on an open brazier.

Vlad the Impaler (the original Dracula), had stakes with rounded ends inserted into his victim's rectum and then had the stake placed in an upright position until the unfortunate died a slow and agonising death. There was no end of the cruelties Man inflicted on his fellow men.

One would have thought that in more civilized societies, these persecutions would have ceased, but as recently as the 1940s the Nazi regime in Germany persecuted the Jewish population, and sent millions of Jews, homosexuals, gypsies, and the mentally handicapped to die in the gas chambers of Auschwitz and other death camps. This included men, women, and little children. All this was done simply because these people did not fit in with the idealistic society the Germans were trying to create. They even went to the extraordinary lengths of starting a program called Lebensborn, to create a super-race of children of purely Aryan descent. This was achieved by accommodating unmarried women of pure Aryan descent in hostels all over the countryside, and having them impregnated by German SS officers and soldiers. The children they produced were indoctrinated in the Nazi philosophy together with other children the Nazis had kidnapped from the various countries they occupied, if they thought these children were of Aryan descent.

What is this resident evil that exists in man's psyche? Looking at it from a religious viewpoint, did God feel that his creation had turned into a Frankenstein monster? He certainly considered that man had been corrupted, and He acted upon this by destroying everyone on Earth in the Flood, except for Noah and his family. In creation theories, everything that God created he considered to be good, as he seemed to want to make a perfect world. Man was probably his first big disappointment!

Purely from a religious perspective, if this life is a testing ground for us humans, and we are given the choice of following the path of good or evil, then our soul has to be judged to determine whether it should re-join the society it came from and become one of God's angels, or be cast into the fires of Hell.

The concept of a soul is a belief in something non-material. Therefore, if it were true it would not be constrained by the laws of physics, so in theory it should be able to travel the length and breadth of the Universe instantly. Consequently, if there is a civilization somewhere in this vast Cosmos where it originated, it is conceivable that it will return there to occupy another body and gain a new identity.

If the philosophies of reincarnation or rebirth are believed, these souls could then return, and enter the body of a newly born baby here on Earth, where it would reside until death. This cycle of reincarnation could be repeated time and time again, until a state of Nirvana is reached, as proposed by many religious theologies.

We have all heard the expression 'starting with a clean slate'. Well, perhaps we are something like a blank slate—our entity that has always existed. After we are born, the slate gets written upon—our life experiences, memories, thoughts, ideas, and aspirations. However, when we die, all this writing is erased and we are just the blank slate again, until we are re-born and start off again in a new life, whereupon the slate is written upon once more. In other words, the real you is the permanent entity—the slate; whereas the writing upon it is temporal and transitory.

Of course, atheists will always argue their case that no gods or deities exist or have ever existed, and that we have no souls or an afterlife. They represent only about 2% of the world's population of 7 billion, and are mainly in the Western world, particularly Europe. They may be right, but are in a small minority. Most cultures do believe in a spiritual life, and in gods and deities, and this conviction seems to be woven into the very fabric of the human psyche. The thought that this brief spell of life on this planet is the be-all and end-all of all existence is an uncomfortable and disturbing one. It would mean that life had no purpose. To simply fade into oblivion after having tasted life seems incomprehensible to many of us.

Atheists can argue that death is akin to periods of unconsciousness, like going under an anaesthetic during the course of an operation, when we are oblivious to the world around us and time seems to stop. But of course, death and unconsciousness are not the same thing, for in an unconscious state, we are still living and breathing, and when we regain consciousness, all our thoughts and memories are intact, much like a computer when it is switched off then restarted has all the information still stored in it. We can argue that before our birth, we did not exist. But who can say for sure that we did not, and simply cannot remember—the slate having been wiped clean? After all, we cannot remember our own babyhood, let alone a previous existence!

This is why the concepts of reincarnation or rebirth are so much more reassuring. They seem to have the advantage of offering us a familiar sort of existence that we enjoy here, something that is in the realms of our experience. Any other sort of afterlife is unimaginable to us, as it is outside our understanding.

In addition, the concept of Karma is a promise of a fruitful life following an unfruitful one, if you have created good Karma. Those of us, who might have lived a life that was

187

unfulfilled, where we were deprived of many of life's pleasures, could be rewarded by a much better and complete life in another birth, if we have lived a worthwhile life or lives previously.

The concept of a soul, or something 'other', is fundamental to most religious belief. However, of course, there is no *evidence* for the existence of a soul. This is where belief in the spiritual and knowledge of the physical part company. Physics will only accept things that can be seen, felt, measured, etc. It cannot do this with the non-physical.

Death is final, and no one has ever returned to give an account of his or her experience. Everyone dies, and no one returns, and this is the great mystery of life.

Where Do I Begin?

There is still some controversy as to when life starts. Some scientists argue that life begins at the moment of conception, when sperm meets ovum. Others claim that life starts later on in pregnancy. There is not yet a clear definition, and this is an important point for medical science and for those pro and anti abortion, as it has all sorts of moral implications—i.e., when can embryos be aborted and when can they be used for medical research?

A normal human pregnancy usually lasts about 38 weeks from fertilisation, and the growing embryo is generally referred to as a foetus after the first 8 weeks from conception. Later on in pregnancy, it is termed a baby. It is a living but not yet breathing thing, as it floats in its sack of embryonic fluids in the dark, warmth, peace, and safety of its mother's womb. In the later stages of pregnancy, it is capable of movement and can probably hear sounds from the outside world. However, it is not until it emerges from the birth canal and enters a world of sound and light that it takes its first breath and awakens to full consciousness. This must be a very stressful and traumatic event for the newly born baby, as its senses awaken, so it is no wonder it greets the world with its cries as it enters this unfamiliar environment. Its next instinct is to seek sustenance by suckling from its mother's breast. Hitherto, all the nourishment it needed was provided through its mother's bloodstream. Now it has to depend on its ability to suckle in order to survive.

Consciousness is a state of mind that philosophers and medical science have been struggling to comprehend. Basically, it can be described as awareness of our surroundings, and the ability to experience and feel. It is literally the stimulation of our senses of sight, sound, touch, taste, and smell. When we are conscious, we are alert to the world around us. However, we are not always in this mental condition, for when we are asleep we are in a semi-conscious state and live in a world of dreams, mostly oblivious to the world around us. However, there remains some residual awareness in this state as we can be woken by, say, a loud noise. It is in this condition that we spend about a third of our lives.

Conversely, unconsciousness is a state of being unaware of anything around us. Fortunately, unconsciousness is a rare experience in our lives, and unless one has to undergo an operation where we are put under a general anaesthetic, we are conscious for most of our lives. In some cases, a person goes into a coma, and can remain unconscious for months or even years in a vegetative state. Hence, it is consciousness that is more significant than perhaps life itself. To be in a constant vegetative state is a living death, and this could last for years owing to life-supporting medical equipment, until our loved ones have to make the terrible decision to switch these off.

Going back to our newly born baby, it takes a few years before it becomes aware of itself. It sees bright objects before itself, and reaches out to touch them; it recognises its mother's smiling face, and gurgles in response; it laughs; it cries. Then as the months go by, it starts to crawl, before taking its first unsteady steps. However, it will not reach a self-conscious state, until it begins to recognise itself in a mirror or begin to blush in embarrassment. The first words of a baby are always a delight to parents, and then the first few words turn to conversation. The learning period goes on for many years, as a child progresses from childhood to adulthood, and is the longest in the animal kingdom. Whereas a baby goat can stand up and start frisking about a few hours after birth, we humans take a much, much longer time to develop.

In the animal kingdom, calves, cubs, kittens, etc., reach adulthood within a few short months, and can mate and reproduce in a relatively short period. Whereas in us humans, it takes several years for our brains to develop as also our bodies, and puberty is generally reached in our unruly teens. When we mature to our adulthood, we progress to middle age and finally to old age when the ability to reproduce ceases. Our lives usually end when we are in our eighties, though some die earlier and some later. Our lifespan largely depends on where we live on this planet. In early times, people rarely lived beyond their sixties.

Strangely, we humans are less familiar to ourselves than to others. Even when we glance at our reflection in a mirror, we are seeing a reverse image of ourselves, and not as others see us. In addition, our voice is unfamiliar to us when we hear ourselves speak in a recording, because we are not used to hearing it outside of our skulls.

What makes me myself, and so distinct and apart from everyone else? It is almost as though we were the driver of a car, occupying and controlling a piece of mechanical machinery, and everything else is on the outside and we are in the inside. Although we can empathise with our fellow humans only through our own human experience, we cannot feel their actual pain or suffer their mental anguish. Our identity and personality is ours and ours alone. We see, we hear, we touch, we smell, we taste and, above everything else, we think. They are our own thoughts and are kept secret from everyone else, unless we care to share them. Our memories are our own, and they go far back into our childhood. We see them like snapshots, and can remember familiar faces almost as accurately as in a photograph.

'I think, therefore I am,' are the famous philosophical words of Rene Descartes to prove that he indeed existed. We humans certainly seem to be endowed with this unique ability to think. An animal, conversely, does not seem to have this ability. They cannot wonder, deliberate, or ponder. They seem to accept the world simply as it is, and not think about it. They also live very much in the present, unlike ourselves who remember the past, and contemplate the future. However, thought is a difficult concept to understand. Biologically, it is neurons circulating around our brains, but a thought, belief, or idea is difficult to explain in physical terms.

The fact that we exist is something of wonderment. Where was I during the aeons before my birth? Did I exist at all or did I exist as something else? If I did not exist, would it matter if the Universe did not exist? In the race to existence, what if I had not been the spermatozoon that fertilized my mother's egg? What if I had been discarded amongst the many millions of my fellow competitors? What has that chance encounter to do with my destiny? Was there a purpose in all of this? These are very thought-provoking questions—the answers to which will forever remain a mystery.

Mind over Matter

Having a mind makes our species so very different from the rest of the animals on this planet. The brain is considered the receptacle for the mind, and although other animals, insects, and fish have a brain, they are thought not to have a mind. The mind gives us the ability to think.

The human brain is the control centre for the body. It communicates with the rest of the body through the spinal cord, which forms part of the nervous system—a very complicated network of nerves. It is through these nerves that our body is able to sense the world around us—sight, sound, smell, taste, and touch. Through the nerves, we feel pain, which though uncomfortable for us, acts as a warning that part of our body is being attacked or threatened. For example, when we burn our finger on a hot stove, the pain we feel makes us immediately aware of this, and we withdraw our finger quickly before it is seriously damaged. All these sensations of pain are registered by the brain. Strangely enough, however, the brain itself is insensitive to pain, and neuro-surgeons can quite easily insert electrodes into the brain of a conscious patient without damaging it or causing any pain. It works something like inserting a knitting needle into a ball of wool, where it can go through without damage.

The brain controls all parts of our body, and is responsible for all movement of our bodily parts. Besides that, it holds all our thoughts, memories, and emotions, and also gives us the ability to speak. It is the receptacle for all knowledge, speech, and language. The brain is made up of trillions of special cells called neurons, and electrical signals are transmitted through these neurons by a very complicated network of connections.

It has always been the conception that the heart holds all our emotions, like love, hate, fear, and courage. This is probably because our heart reacts to these feelings. But it is really the brain where all these emotions are held. The heart is merely a pump, albeit a very efficient one, that delivers blood to all parts of our body. Our brain needs a constant supply of oxygen-containing blood, and if it is deprived of this for only a few seconds, it can lead to unconsciousness, whereas if we tie up one of our fingers and deprive it of a blood-supply, it can continue functioning for several minutes. Not so the brain. If it is deprived of oxygen for only seven minutes or so, it can lead to severe brain damage and even death. The brain also uses up an enormous amount of glucose in the blood and if there is not sufficient glucose, sufferers of diabetes can go into a diabetic coma, which is sometimes fatal.

In almost all animal species, the brain is always contained in the head, which is separated from the rest of the body. The head is where our most sensitive organs, like the eyes, nose, mouth, and ears are located. If it were possible to separate the head from the body and provide all the necessary nutrients for it to function, it might still have the ability to see, hear, and taste. It would be a thinking head! Conversely, if our brain dies, the rest of the body dies with it.

Diseases of the brain are among the most serious medical conditions. These can take the form of dementia or Alzheimer's disease, which are becoming very common-place among the elderly now-a-days. Here, memory loss and the inability to recognise your nearest and dearest is the saddest thing. Usually such a person has to be admitted to a care home, as it becomes increasingly difficult for relatives or close friends to give them all the care, support, and attention they need.

Motor-neurone disease is also completely disabling. This is when motor neurones, the cells that control essential voluntary muscles, are progressively destroyed. Sufferers of this disease can become so disabled as to lose the use of all their limbs, and even speech, as in the case of the eminent astrophysicist Stephen Hawking, who has to use a computer-generated speech device in order to communicate. However, though his body is completely impaired, his mind is totally functional, and his scientific genius has enabled him to write such books as *A Brief History of Time*.

Epilepsy is also a serious mental condition that is characterised by seizures. These seizures can cause the sufferer to bouts of violent shaking. It is sometimes described as an electrical storm going through the brain. Such seizures can be brought on by simple things like flashing lights, which is why there are so many warnings on television programs and films that some scenes may contain flashing images.

Mental retardation is also a very sad condition, especially since it occurs mainly in childhood. The parents of such a handicapped child, although they may love him or her dearly, never have the fulfilment of seeing their loved one develop into a fully independent and competent adult, and have to devote the rest of their lives to caring for and supporting their child.

Then there are so many other psychological disorders, like schizophrenia, where the person suffers from delusions, paranoia, or worse, resulting in the individual sometimes becoming so deranged as to commit terrible crimes. Some psychopaths turn into serial killers or maniacs.

The brain plays a very important role in establishing our identity. There are some individuals that have a split personality, i.e. they take on the role of two different people, or multiple personalities. This is medically known as Dissociative Identity Disorder (DID) or Multiple Personality Disorder (MPD).

There are also individuals who believe they are of the wrong sex, believing they are women trapped in men's bodies or vice-versa. These are termed 'transsexuals', and some go to the lengths of undergoing operations on their genitalia and the use of drugs in an attempt to alter their gender. The brain seems to determine your sexual identity and not, for example, the way you are brought up—as a boy or as a girl.

There was the tragic case of David Reimer, a Canadian man who was born a healthy male, but when a circumcision operation went wrong and his penis was destroyed, his psychologist, John Money, tried an experiment by having the boy brought up as a girl, in the hope that this would establish his sexual identity. However, the experiment was not a success, and Reimer failed to ever identify himself as a female. In adulthood, he reverted to his male gender, but due to severe depression eventually committed suicide.

Homosexuality, considered a sin and unnatural in the past, is now becoming much more socially acceptable, though there is still some debate on the issue, especially by some sections of the Church. Some approve, while some do not. But happily, it was decriminalised by the law in England back in the 1960s, and since then people have been much more forthright in declaring themselves gay, and leading a fulfilled life. One can only recall the sad case of the eminent author and poet Oscar Wilde, in the latter part of the 19th century, when he was accused of sodomy, and tried and jailed for his so-called crime. Fortunately, we live in a far more tolerant society today.

Sexual fetishes also play a role in our sexual preferences. Here a person receives sexual arousal from a specific situation or object, as for example having the partner wear a particular garment in the course of sexual activity. Some individuals have a fetish for rubber or leather; some have a fetish for feet, and as the saying goes, 'It's all in the mind.'

We humans also suffer from a host of behavioural problems, like obsessive-compulsive disorder, depression, anxiety, anorexia nervosa, etc. We also suffer from various phobias, like acrophobia (fear of heights), arachnophobia (fear of spiders), claustrophobia (fear of confined spaces), and nosophobia (fear of contracting disease). The list goes on and on.

Coming back to the physical: damage to the spinal cord, which is an extension of the brain, can cause severe disability. Although this is well-protected by the vertebrae of the spine, it can become damaged in accidents, as happened to film actor Christopher Reeve when he fell off a horse in a riding accident. The former star of Superman was completely immobilised by this tragic accident, and had to spend the rest of his life in a specially designed wheelchair, equipped with breathing apparatus to enable him to breathe and talk.

Strokes are another calamitous event that can strike people, mostly the elderly. This happens when a blood vessel in the brain ruptures, and forms a blood clot, blocking off a portion of the brain. This can result in paralysis, and loss of memory and speech. The severity of the damage largely relies on the severity and location of the stroke, and in many cases, the person can partially recover over the course of time.

We cannot live without a brain. Besides the heart, it is the most vital of our vital organs. Although we have a better understanding of how the brain works, it still holds many mysteries which medical science has not yet been able to unravel. But at least it is something physical, which we can see, feel, and analyse with medical appliances like scanners and such.

The mind is very different. It cannot be seen or touched, as it is something non-physical. It cannot even be read by others, and is accessible only to ourselves. It makes up our whole personality—who we are, and the thoughts, memories, and emotions we hold. For example, how can we express an idea in physical terms? It has no substance. Although we all have the same sort of brain, we are completely different individuals when it comes to our personality.

Of course, the mind can be analysed and tested by psychologists by asking probing questions. Our knowledge, memories, skills, and abilities can also be tested by another analytical mind.

In the early part of the 20th century, psychologists like Sigmund Freud and William James, developed influential theories regarding the nature of the human mind. Freud particularly, employed therapeutic techniques where patients revealed their thoughts without reservation, and he concluded that many of his patients' problems had associations with their early relationship with their mother, and their childhood sexuality.

Hypnosis was another technique hypnotists employed to try and delve into the human mind. Here the patient is put into a trance-like state and becomes very sensitive to suggestion, which the hypnotist uses, often inducing his patient to reveal hidden memories that may have happened in the patient's childhood. In some cases, the hypnotist has even induced his patient to go beyond his childhood and into a previous life. How reliable these techniques are is open to question, but there have been some interesting cases where the patient has recalled a past life when he was a different person living in a different time. This has encouraged belief in reincarnation and rebirth.

Magicians can also use hypnosis in their performance of tricks. This often happens on stage. For example, the magician may ask for a volunteer to join him on the stage, and put him or her in a hypnotic trance. He may, for example, suggest to the volunteer that the number seven does not exist, and he then asks him or her to count their fingers. The look of bewilderment on the volunteer's face is something to behold, when they try counting their fingers, and find they have eleven!

Our minds can also be quite easily fooled. We can suffer hallucinations that can be brought on by drugs like LSD. This tricking of the mind can be achieved with quite simple experiments, like crossing your fingers then rolling them over a marble. You feel two marbles, whereas in reality there is only one. Figments of the imagination are also quite common. We all may have had the experience of being deluded into believing something that does not exist. Or sometimes what we see cannot be interpreted by the mind. The eyes and the brain usually work together, so what we see we interpret. However, sometimes this is not the case, and our eyes tell us one thing and our brain another. For example, when a train standing alongside yours, starts to move off, you are quite often fooled into thinking it is your train that has started. It is only when the brain kicks in and tells you that you are in fact stationary, that you realize your mistake.

A trick ventriloquists' use is to talk without moving their lips, and operate the mouth of their dummy to move instead. This fools you into believing that it is the dummy that is talking and not the ventriloquist. These are just a couple of examples to show how easily your mind can be fooled.

The brain and the mind will continue to mystify and amaze us. In the meantime, medical science and psychologists and such are trying to unravel some of its mysteries, and some day may be able to gain a better understanding of how they work together and what makes up our psyche.

Final Destination

Particularly in the New Testament of the Bible, we are given the promise of everlasting life. But what does this mean? Does it mean that this life is some sort of spiritual life, or does it mean a physical sort of existence like the one we enjoy here?

There are popular misconceptions about Heaven. To some, it is visualised to exist in the sky, where angels sit on clouds playing their harps, or Saint Peter meeting you at the Pearly Gates. This would seem a very boring sort of place. Very little is told to us about this eventual residence for us humans in the afterlife. Jesus mentions that in his Father's house are many 'mansions'. This could be interpreted to mean locations, dwelling places, and abodes and such. But at the very best, this is a very vague description. To try to trick him, a scenario was put to him by the Sadducees about a woman who had been married seven times in succession, each of her former spouses having died before the next. They asked him whose wife she would be in Heaven. To this, Jesus replied that there were no marriages recognised in Heaven, but that anyone entering would simply become as one of the angels, and be given a new body and a new identity.

This idea of all of us becoming angels in Heaven contradicts the concept that after our death we would be reunited with our family and loved ones, and recognise them as such. Therefore, reunion with our nearest and dearest is a popular misconception. It is never mentioned anywhere in the Bible that such a reunification would ever happen in our afterlife.

Being given a new body and identity seems to make better sense, as there would be an awful mix-up if we were to reunite with a grandparent who had died at a younger age than ourselves, or a baby that had died before it had the chance to develop a personality. Would it remain as a baby throughout eternity? So could this concept of being given another body and identity mean a physical sort of existence in the afterlife?

Could this be seen as a Karmic interpretation—where we go back to our true identity in the afterlife? As Shakespeare put it, 'All the world is a stage,' and we are simply actors, playing out our various roles. Does this mean that we come back to Earth as another player in another role in another play? Perhaps this is how we could recognise our nearest and dearest as their original entities in Heaven, and thus meet up with them again as our fellow actors who played their part in our life on Earth.

This raises the question of re-incarnation, which is mainly excluded from the modern Judeo-Christian-Islamic faith, but is the philosophy of many other faiths, especially in India. After all, if we spend just one lifetime in this world, would it be enough to judge whether we are good or evil or would we be given a second chance to prove ourselves? If life on this planet is some sort of test, one lifetime would not be enough to test us in all aspects of human experience. For example, if we were to be tested in a life of great wealth and power, how would we behave in a life of extreme deprivation and poverty?

Originating in India, reincarnation or rebirth is fundamental to the Hindu, Jain, Buddhist, and Sikh philosophies. It is a concept that the soul or spirit or karmic energy, after leaving our bodies in death, is continuously re-born in a cycle of incarnations, which is determined by our Karma—how well or how badly you lived your life. These incarnations can be of any form of life—insect, animal, fish, or fowl. Your soul progresses through these cycles of birth and re-birth, and you go up the scale depending on how well you have performed in your previous existence. Reincarnation is a concept that is gaining popularity in many Western cultures in recent decades. Unlike the vague references to an afterlife in the Judeo-Christian-Islamic faiths, it at least offers some sort of expectation that we can return for another spell on familiar Earth, albeit as a different entity, and live another life—hopefully a better one if our Karma was good.

There are some vague references to reincarnation in the Bible. Jesus was once asked if John the Baptist was the prophet Elijah returned from the dead.

Belief in everlasting life in Heaven or eternal damnation in the fires of Hell was a very persuasive argument for leading a godly life and seeking repentance for any of our sins, and the Church used this to very good effect! However, blind faith in one's religious beliefs was responsible for great acts of courage in olden days, because the physical life seemed less important than the spiritual one to many of the faithful.

Today the opposite is true, and our life on Earth is of prime importance as belief in the existence of an all knowing and all loving God is becoming less convincing. Many are questioning that if such a God exists, why does He allow such terrible events to happen to us and not intervene, as He may have done in the past? In our own experience, we would never allow even our pet cat to suffer, let alone one of our loved ones. So why does He, the God of Love, allow us to suffer hardship, pain, and death? Whatever, He is certainly becoming more remote and less intervening. Nevertheless, in times of trouble, most people turn to God when all hope seems to be lost, and this seems to be part of the natural human psyche.

In recent years, there have been a number of incidents where seriously ill people, or those having been pronounced dead in hospital but then resuscitated, have encountered near-death experiences. In such episodes, the person experiences levitation—the leaving of the body—and can see themselves on the bed or operating table, with medical staff in attendance. A feeling of serenity, security, and warmth is reported, and they often see a bright light at the end of a tunnel, which they seem to be drawn towards. Then suddenly, they have the sensation of being pulled back into their body, and return to consciousness. There are also instances of people having out-of-body experiences during sleep, where they have a sensation of leaving their bodies and floating around the room, but are suddenly pulled back into themselves on awakening.

Death will come to all of us eventually. That is the only certainty we have in our human experience: that it will all come to an end someday. For the more fortunate, they will live a healthy and fruitful life and live well into old age, until their vital organs fail, and they die peacefully. The less fortunate may die tragically, sometimes in their youth or even childhood. However, thanks to modern medicine, more people are surviving to a ripe old age, and infant mortality is becoming less and less frequent. One can only realise how many children died in their childhood, by visiting Victorian cemeteries.

In many ways, our journey through life resembles a journey on a train. You are sitting with your back towards the engine. You see through your window all that is passing by. You cannot see what is coming towards you. Passengers leave and join the carriage at intervals. Eventually you come to your station. You alight from the train. Is your journey now at an end? Or do you wait on the platform for another train to come, which you board to continue on another journey to your final destination?

Other books by James Sinclair

Over Our Heads
Don't Water the Marigolds
In the Shade of the Shamiana

25652303R00120

Made in the USA
Columbia, SC
06 September 2018